MODERN FRENCH PAINTERS

By

JAN GORDON

With Forty Illustrations

New Edition

LONDON : JOHN LANE THE BODLEY HEAD LTD.
NEW YORK : DODD, MEAD AND COMPANY

First Published in 1923
Reprinted . . . 1926
New Edition . . 1929
Revised Edition . 1936

MADE AND PRINTED IN GREAT BRITAIN BY WILLIAM CLOWES AND SONS, LIMITED
LONDON AND BECCLES

TO

MY FRIENDS

DORIS AND ASHLEY SMITH

UNDER WHOSE HOSPITABLE ROOF WAS BEGUN THAT
OTHER BOOK WHICH EVENTUALLY DEVELOPED INTO
THIS VOLUME

INTRODUCTION

THIS book was designed with a definite purpose. It was planned to be an introduction, and a persuasive introduction, to the puzzling problems of what is called " Modern Art." I wished to provide for the honest inquirer a dim glimmer of light through the murky road which leads to understanding and enjoyment, although I am well aware that no book or reading matter can be a substitute for the more serious exercise of looking at pictures. The honest man with artistic leanings has been puzzled, perplexed, and exasperated. If he tried to help himself with works published on the subject he was often even more puzzled and perplexed, as " Modern Art " invented for itself a jargon, half philosophical, half mystic, which became more difficult to understand than the works which it was meant to elucidate. And since, after eleven years, the demand for this book is still enough to warrant a fourth reprinting, I may assume that the purpose of the work has to some extent been achieved.

This book was an attempt to put into plainly intelligible language the ideas behind and the developments of the varied phases of " Modern Art." I wished that my readers should understand what I was saying, even if they did not agree with me. And in the persual of this task I would like to acknowledge the assistance of the two friends whose names appear on the dedicatory page. They patiently listened to the progress of the work chapter by chapter ; if they deemed any phrase too recondite or too technical it was struck out and simplified. In fact, I may say that the material was filtered through their brains, and as they were exactly the kind of readers whom I was trying to reach, I was able to flatter myself that I had at least produced the kind of book that I had planned to make at the outset. Nevertheless, a few of the higher critics, notably in America, have blamed me for not having produced the very kind of thing I was trying to avoid. But this book, being intended for those whom Mr. Wells has called the broad-brows, could naturally not satisfy the high-brows. A few other critics blamed me because I have refused to take sides and brandish a cudgel furiously for one kind or other of the extremely varied and often contradictory exponents of this " Modern Art." And yet, after all, were you listening-in at a football match, you would hardly be grateful to find that the announcer was violently partizan. His business is to sit on the fence, no matter what his private sympathies may be. So, amongst these conflicting developments, I have wished to remain neutral. Had I tried to influence the reader's private judgment to one side or the other, my purpose would again have been defeated.

For in spite of this book of analysis and explanation, one central fact remains. The final value of a picture depends not at all on the theories which produced it, but upon the personal and innate power of the artist. A poor painter could not produce a masterpiece, even though he had the colours of the rainbow and the logic of Einstein at his disposal, while a genius will do wonders with a piece of torn wall-paper and a burnt match end. And yet an understanding of the leading ideas may help the onlooker to a more rapid appreciation, and with this purpose in mind the book has been written. The artist himself is often pushed forward instinctively ; the theories which explain what he has done are often invented, not previous to the production, but afterwards, either by himself or by the critics trying to account for him. In fact, we may assert that with the more valuable contributors to the " Modern " movement the Art came first and the theory afterwards. Artists are seldom logicians in words ; they think with the ends of their paint brushes.

It is amongst the minor movements that you will find the majority of those who theorize first, and then struggle to fill the sausage-skin of their theory with adequate meat of pictorial accomplishment. Many such have risen and faded out beneath the slow, strong, general rise of the greater " Modern " movement. Such little agitations are clamorous during their short existences. They fill the cafés of Montparnasse with painters who dispute far more vigorously than they paint. They form bands of professional despisers, and thus often cloud the mind of the honest inquirer with a suspicion of the whole movement.

This book reviews the development from the beginnings of Neo-impressionism until the climax of Cubism and the outbreak of the Great War. Almost simultaneously with this last the surge of new experiment dwindles. When the editors suggested a new printing the question arose whether any serious revision of the text was necessary. But on page 174 I had ventured to prophecy that, " The public may expect no new shocks for a very long while." This was in harmony with the ideas about Art and Civilisation described in Chapter VII. I am pleased to say that in the interval, allowing for the intention and the limits of the book, no considerable alteration is needed. The only addition we could make would be a list of the new talent which has since arisen, but all of it is within the lines already indicated in this volume, and as we are here concerned rather with the ideas than with the men, such a list would only contradict our central purpose.

Cubism still seems the final stumbling-block before the intelligent amateur. And yet if he but looks intelligently about him he will find that of all the new practices developed within the last fifty years, Cubism has had the widest popular spread. It can be said almost to permeate the whole of our modern artistic environment. One cannot open a paper without finding advertisements frankly cubistic. It appears in our architecture, in our dress materials, in our furniture, in our decoration, in our photography, in our shop windows. In fact, this movement, which less than thirty years ago caused the Paris critics to gnash their teeth in fury, has become the background of so much of our visible existence that we should feel a strange deprivation if it were magically withdrawn. Therefore, however much we may feel antagonistic to the cubistic work and ideas of Picasso or of Braque as painters, we should hesitate before we venture to condemn men whose practices have had so sweeping and so world-wide an influence.

JAN GORDON.

PARIS,
June, 1929.

LONDON,
May, 1936.

CONTENTS

LIST OF ILLUSTRATIONS

IN COLOUR

xiii

IN BLACK AND WHITE

MODERN FRENCH PAINTERS

MODERN FRENCH PAINTERS

CHAPTER I

THE LANGUAGES OF ART

A TRAVELLER who wishes to make his way through a piece of country unknown to him, instead of plunging boldly into the first path which seems to lead in the right direction, may go out of his way somewhat and ascend a hill from the summit of which he can get a general survey of the country he would cross. The time lost may be time gained, for from thence he may see a path which, starting in an unlooked-for direction, will lead him to his destination more quickly than if he had taken the apparently straight road.

We may equally at the outset of this inquiry clamber a little amongst the shrubbery of a country which is not our proper province. We may make a short tour into some aspects of literature—particularly aspects of prose—from whence we may spy the openings of the road which we have to follow if we would come to a common-sense under-standing of the most recent developments of the art of painting.

Words are the materials out of which literature is made. These words are a human invention with which to exchange ideas, one person with another. Everybody speaks prose, a faculty which has been learned so unconsciously that one is scarcely conscious of having learned it at all. It has been proved that words have no peculiar virtues apart from the ideas which they express, and the whole idea underlying the invention of words and of grammar is clarity. The

B

chief idea of literature is to express oneself clearly, and anybody who can thus write clearly is writing good literature. Literature is a means for conveying to others thoughts which they could not find for themselves, and the beauty of the literature depends largely upon the beauty of the thought. The grammar of a language has not been made for the purpose of beauty, but for utility alone, and in this way differs from the grammar of painting or of music upon which beauty depends in the prime instance. Literature has three qualities with which to produce art; these are (1) beauty of thought, (2) clarity of expression, (3) beauty of language. Without these three, writing remains merely a means of exchanging ideas, it does not become a work of art.

A piece of writing in a foreign language is to us a piece of foolishness until we have learned to understand the language in which it is written. The two prime qualities which make up art are lacking to us, while even the third, which depends more upon the ear alone than upon the understanding, has little virtue, or even beauty, until the intelligence shines its light upon the music of the language. As music alone it is monotonous, and if the language contains unusual sounds it may appear ugly.

"Wer reitet so spät durch Nacht und Wind?
Es ist der Vater mit seinem Kind"

must be hideous and can have no beauty of expression nor music of words to, say, an unlettered Italian.

We will acknowledge that it were mere impertinence to criticize a foreign work of literature as long as we cannot understand the language in which it is written. But, nevertheless, the three qualities by which written art is made are the same no matter what the language employed. Provided that we work within these limits we may say what we like. But in order to fulfil the second of the qualities we cannot depart very widely from the rules of grammar, nor can we change the meaning of words. Language is so artificial a thing that if its rules are disdained the thought which the author would express is not handed on to his audience. Grammar is as artificial as is the coinage system ; neither can be depreciated without losing the means of exchange. We cannot follow Humpty-Dumpty's method, however fascinating it may appear. The discoveries of literature are discoveries in thought, discoveries in subtlety and in music of expression. But the bigger construction rules remain stable, changing perhaps slowly with use, but so gradually that it is almost impossible to say at what time any stated change begins.

Language imposes as rigid a method of expression as, say, that which Egyptians imposed upon their sculptors. The latter had, as it were, a grammar of sculpture. Within that grammar the artist was allowed liberty. The differences of technique which exist between two such writers as Defoe and Meredith are not greater than those which exist between Hokusai and Outamaro or between a middle and a late period of Greek statuary.

From a certain point of view painting and music are more instinctive arts than literature. The child delights in colour and in musical sounds before words have any meaning to it. It is imagined that no particular learning is needed to gain an appreciation of either art, for the delight in both comes by means of the senses, which are susceptible to education only in moderate degrees. The delight in literature comes largely through the understanding—a small part only, harmony of language, being purely of the senses.

It would be possible for an ingenious man to invent a language for himself. He might then write works of art in this language, but the work would remain of no value as art until another person had learned the language. Homer would have no value as art if the secret of Greek had been lost. No human production can have value as art or as beauty if the language in which it is expressed cannot be understood. If I remark : " Nye manye smertee od glahdee eema," or, perhaps, " Marcoussis arpiteh dye patra deressis," or, " Tye Tamee Te niye te ne-eh," I could ask the majority of my readers if these sentences were beautiful sense or idiotic nonsense without risking an authoritative reply. If we choose to perceive a certain beauty in one of them, it is clear, however, that this particular form of beauty could not be continued for more than twenty lines without the risk of sending the listener to sleep. The same can be found to hold in one of the parallel arts of music or of painting, more obviously perhaps in the former. Chinese music has a language quite different from that of European, and to the average Westerner is unmitigated noise. We can come even closer to home and find in the style of Spanish gipsy singing a musical art of a different nature from that of ordinary European singing. This art, which has great charm and a voice production peculiar to itself, can only be appreciated by learning to hear it properly. Recently an exhibition of Spanish singing in London moved the audiences to mirth and the critics to derision ; but, curiously enough, a similar effect would be produced upon a Spanish village audience by an operatic singer.

Thus, though we may admit easily that there are in foreign languages forms of art to which the understanding does not react, we are slow to recognize that there are also forms of art which the senses do not recognize. The average literary critic would be slow to criticize a book presented to him written in a tongue which he did not understand ; but of the popular London musical critics I believe only one, when suddenly confronted with Spanish Flamenco singing, had the wit to perceive that here was a musical language which he did not understand and which was therefore not to be judged by his standards. The English yokel used to have the conviction that English is the only possible language, and foreign languages are foolish ; and even in English he had a preference for his own dialect. We have become settled in the idea that there is but one language in art, and we tend to look upon the arts of other civilizations with some of the condescension of the yokel's attitude towards French. This was more true a hundred years ago than it is now. We have to some extent begun to learn the foreign languages of art, but the comments of the visitors at the National Gallery on the Italian primitives, who are the founders of our own artistic language, show a strange likeness to the comments of a schoolboy of eighteen who is shown Chaucer for the first time.

The three examples given above show that when the understanding cannot play its part, the senses may be prevented from giving pleasure. It might be imagined that since painting and music are principally enjoyed by means of the senses, that this blocking on the part of the intelligence would not take place; that the senses would rule and guide the intelligence. This would be the case if we allowed the senses the upper hand. If we were content simply to look at painting or listen to music, allowing its message to touch us at first by feeling only, we would get a more just estimate of the various kinds of art than we do. But this is difficult. It is a more easy way to recognize that there are several different languages, and to suspend judgment till the understanding of the new language has been reached. This can only be done by a certain amount of study.

In *The Soul of Man under Socialism*, Wilde says that a man who comes to a new work of art " with authority " can get nothing from it; that is, a man who expects to see a certain kind of effect will get nothing if the work is conceived otherwise. We can exaggerate this statement into this: that a man who comes to a work in French expecting it to be written in English, and who determines to judge it as if it were written in English, will get no good from the work—which is clear. It is equally true that the man who comes to a Post-Impressionist picture expecting it to be painted in the language of Velazquez or Rembrandt will get no benefit. The person who instinctively does not like Post-Impressionist pictures is in the position of the Italian peasant who, instinctively also, does not like the sound of German poetry.

There is, however, an essential difference between the arts of literature and of painting or music. Literature is the setting down of ideas, and even books of deliberate nonsense have a fantastic glamour of sense which makes them incredibly credible. In the expression of the idea there is an amazing flexibility. We can handle the symbols of words in a hundred diverse fashions to create the same sense out of them. That is, the thing expressed and the means of expression are to some extent separate from one another. This is less true of poetry than of prose ; but, in prose writings, even an able translation into another tongue can give the larger virtues of a foreign author ; indeed, a translation is as much like the original as a good photographic reproduction is of a picture ; in each the intimate colour is sacrificed, but the major virtues remain. But in painting or in music no paraphrase is possible, change but one colour in a painting or but one chord in a theme and the significance is altered. Indeed the musical variations of the sonata show how the same idea undergoes transformation by differences of treatment. In painting and in music the idea *is* the treatment. There is no suspicion of separability.

The public has, on the whole, quarrelled with painters far more than with writers, and these quarrels usually spring out of this unity or laxity of idea and treatment. The reasons for quarrel are, in general, four. First, quarrels about public morality ; secondly, quarrels about human vanity ; thirdly, quarrels about presentation of fact ; fourthly, quarrels about methods of presentation—or technique. In painting, the public has had quarrels on all four heads with artists. Limiting ourselves always to the European or scientific school, as we may call that development which stretches from Giotto to the Impressionist—for reasons which will appear later—in morality it has quarrelled with Manet (" Olympia," " Déjeuner sur l'herbe," etc.) ; in vanity it has quarrelled with Rembrandt or with Millet ; in presentation of fact it has quarrelled with Corot, with Delacroix, with Turner, and a host of others ; and in technique it has quarrelled with Millet, with Delacroix, with Manet, with Monet and his followers, etc. On the part of literature, covering a similar period, one finds only two causes of quarrel : first, on the score of morality such as with Flaubert or Ibsen or Baudelaire ; secondly, on the score of vanity as with Zola. Arguments concerning presentation of fact and concerning methods of presentation are rare. The reason for the lack of contest between public and author on these latter two points is easy to find. In the first the public mind lacks sufficient imagination to translate an author's facts into reality; it can perceive such an obvious mistake as Sancho Panza's donkey being stolen in one chapter and Sancho riding upon it in the next; but more subtle misstatements it cannot check, it has no training in accuracy of mental perception, and in dreams itself it wanders in such fantastic impossibilities that the imagination is always ready to admit anything short of purely obvious mistakes. In the second count, the public cannot as a rule perceive change of technique, as long as technique remains within certain limits. Differences of technique are more difficult to perceive in writing than in painting because the effect must be cumulative, and the mind must gather up evidence until there is sufficient, while in painting the evidence is all presented at once. But the rules of grammar inflict a restraint which at once sets a model. It is as hard for the average reader spontaneously to perceive differences in style between two writers as it would be for him to notice the differences in style between Watteau and Fragonard, or between Reynolds and Romney. Also the flexibility of the literary medium allows an expression of the most contrasting ideas to be made without alteration of the idiom. But, in painting, idiom and meaning are indissolubly united. For instance, the idea expressed in Egyptian statuary is man as god. The Egyptian statues are not clumsy efforts of a people who could not do otherwise, they are deliberate efforts of an attempt to convey a certain order of truth, the presentation of the superman. When the Egyptian wishes to present man as man, he humanizes his technique. The Grecian technique aims at the glorification of man, of presenting God as man; thus it is the reverse of Egyptian. The Gothic would present the spiritual rising out of the material.

We may then understand change in the technique of painting as change of language forced on the painter because the ideas which he wishes to express can only be expressed by the form he is using. If we consider these idioms as separate foreign languages which have to be studied, and which necessarily contain no beauty until the language has been mastered, much of the difficulty presented by modern manifestations of art will dwindle away.

In the history of the arts of painting we may roughly select the following as the principal *idioms :*

  The Babylonian
  The Egyptian
  The Chinese
  The Greek
  The Islamic
  The Indian
  The Negro
  The Byzantine
  The Gothic.

Each of these is a different idiom of the art of painting—with dialects or sub-idioms—and each represents a different development of man with his different civilization and ideals.   Each had a permanency proportionate to the permanency of the civilization it decorated ; and each requires a separate study in order to be properly appreciated.   Each gains in artistic interest if the mental outlook which produced it is comprehended.   There is, however, a shorthand method of studying languages, which is employed by philologists—whose nature forces them to study languages—which is to divide languages into families ; so that one discovers that all languages spring from very few ancestors.   For instance, almost all the languages of Europe spring from the family called Indo-Germanic ; that is, they have a large number of things in common. When the philologist has learned the characteristics of the Indo-Germanic, he has already a large amount of data concerning almost all the languages of Europe, and has lessened by that amount the labour in acquiring any new one.   This is also true of painting.

There are certain root ideas beneath all varieties of the art of painting, and if one grasps these ideas the difficulty of appreciating any particular idiom is considerably lessened.   What these root ideas are will appear in time.

Following after the Gothic comes a period which I have called the European period, and which represents the time which elapsed between Giotto and the Impressionists. But it might have other names, it might be called the " nature " idiom or the " scientific " idiom, since it is characterized by what may be called a scientific curiosity in the physical appearance of nature, and comes to an end as soon as that inquiry is exhausted. As the other idioms corresponded to the permanency of their peoples, so does this scientific idiom, it changes its dialect and develops with the development of civilization. As it develops, man's vision of nature develops.

It may seem an absurd statement to make, that man did not always see " Nature " as he sees it now. Absurd, and probably from one point of view untrue ; but there is a difference between seeing and perceiving ; just as there is a difference between imagining and expressing.

The eye is a kind of camera. The rays of light passing into it stimulate nerves which carry a message to the brain, and the brain projects an image which we call nature. The world which we see is projected by us as by a magic lantern ; this must be clearly understood. In a certain disease of vision, the two eyes lose parallelism and we get a double vision of nature, one imposed on the other as if two magic lanterns were shining the same picture on the same sheet with the pictures overlapping. We do not normally recognize that the visions of sleep and the visions of wakefulness are due to the same cause—irritation of the optic nerve. If, however, we remember that vision lies in the brain, not in the eye, we can understand the development of the vision of nature by art. We do not perceive what is, but what the brain is looking for—or, rather, for general use we do not perceive with any clearness at all.

It is always difficult for the untrained mind to analyse or to present its thoughts accurately. How often do we have thoughts or impressions which seem quite vivid until we attempt to put them into language. At once they grow indefinite. But imagine that these could be put into language for us by a diviner. Then these ideas would remain with us clear and precise and we could give expression to them ourselves. The perception of nature's appearance is as vague in the natural man as are his thoughts. He sees clearly what he has specialized himself to see—the Indian tracker who can tell from the grass how many foes have passed that road receives on the retina no more than the ordinary man—but outside of his specialized vision his perceptions are vague and indefinite.

Ask the ordinary man to draw from nature a tin pail. He will probably make this sort of figure. He is aware of the opening

because he can see the inside; he sees the curves of the top edge because he must account for his vision of the interior, he is also aware of the slopes of the sides. But he does not *perceive* the rounded ends of the ellipse, and his mind agrees that the pail stands flat on the ground. These two shapes he takes for granted, that is, they are seen but not perceived. But when the real appearance of these two facts is pointed out to him, he does not again make the same mistake : what was formerly invisible now is visible.

The history of European art is a history of the discovery of the reproduction of natural facts. When Whistler says that nature imitates art, he means merely that we do not become consciously aware of many of nature's aspects until more perceptive vision has pointed them out. The painter has been shaping nature for us : and when Vasari praises Uccello for his veracity to nature he is but telling the truth as he knows it. What to us now is the primitive grasping at realistic appearances was to his own century the very mirror of reality.

It will be noticed that at the opening of the European school a host of new and diverse visions of nature are acceptable to the public. Fra Angelico, Botticelli, Uccello, Piero della Francesca, Pisanello, Raphael, Titian, each has a personal vision not only different in technique, but in fact—each is hailed as a master, each as a truth-teller. The vision of nature was still in a fluid state, men's minds were not yet fixed upon any particular aspect. Even the vision of Velazquez and of El Greco was passed over in a land where there was little tradition of art, and when the consciousness of nature had not yet become fixed into rules. The innovations of Watteau— forerunner of the Impressionists—were acceptable partly because he had enclosed his new technique in an old convention, and partly because of his subtle flattery. But the return of David and of Ingres refixed the vision which had developed from the Renaissance. Thus a certain definite teaching of a particular aspect of nature contrives, with time, to influence the conscious idea of nature—one gets a preconceived idea of nature and, as far as one perceives nature at all, perceives her in that mould. Nature becomes no longer vision, but dogma. When this point is reached we get a sudden resistance to the acceptance of new truths about nature.

This explains the outbursts which arose over the work of Corot, Millet and Delacroix in France, of Constable and Turner in England. To-day it seems incredible that Constable's pictures were considered too green ; that he had to place an old violin upon a lawn to show a connoisseur that landscape was not, in nature, the tint of a Stradivarius.

The study of nature comes to a natural climax in two ways : first, exhaustion of the visual method and, secondly, invention of a mechanical method—the photograph. The visual examination of nature comes to an end with Manet, and by a natural path develops into a study of the means by which nature is visible, that is, light. We can follow the steps thus. The first painters record external fact, beginning with man and gradually including other variations of nature ; in Chardin's still lives we have already reached nature with humanity left out : this is pushed farther until we are forced to an analysis of the means by which this external nature is perceived. This stage is Impressionism. The next stage is also a natural development. From the ways in which we perceive we pass to an examination of the thing *which perceives*, that is, man. This is self-analysis. This stage is Post-Impressionism, as it has been called.

Analysis of the means of vision cannot be pursued without coming into contact with the processes of representation, so Post-Impressionism becomes not only conscious of how it understands nature, but also of how works of art are made.   It begins to analyse the subconscious from both aspects, and its work must be appreciated from this standpoint.   It no longer pretends to represent external nature as the average man sees it, it tries to represent effects which nature produces in the inner consciousness.

One has been asked why not go on in the old road?   Why not be content to continue that matter-of-fact representation of external fact which was so easy to understand and under which we had so much pleasure in eating our dinners?   The answer is that one cannot stand still.   It is contrary to the laws of nature.   There is no such thing as lack of change.   The mountain is falling into the valley, the earth never travels the same course twice, history, in spite of the old saw, never repeats itself.   The artist is man brought to the highest point of sensitiveness to life.   How, then, cannot he be the most ready to respond to the law of nature?

CHAPTER II

IMPRESSIONISM AND NEO-IMPRESSIONISM

RUSKIN has said as many true things about art as perhaps any other single man; it is unfortunate that so many of his truths were packed into a chariot which was going in the wrong direction, and that some even were dragged along behind in spite of themselves. But Ruskin's truths have been almost overlooked, while his cult of the " nature " idiom (often wrongly understood) has done much to deter the advance of pictorial appreciation in England. The great stumbling-block in the way of understanding of the art of to-day lies in the mistaken theory that art must copy nature; must, that is, copy an almost dogmatic representation of external nature. Ruskin, however, himself says " good art rarely imitates; it usually only describes or explains." Let us consider the last part of the statement. An explanation is not a description, nor is a description a statement of external fact. When one says that water is a combination of hydrogen and oxygen, both of which are gases, this gives no picture of water; when Stevenson describes Villon, the mediæval poet, by remarking that " the wolf and the pig struggled in his face," he is creating physical impossibilities. The one is explanation at one process below the fact, the other description at three thoughts away from the fact. Each is only possible as description or explanation, because the reader takes a certain mental step, or series of steps along with the writer. It is unnecessary for Stevenson to say: " There were certain indications in his face of a struggle between two forces, one of which by its rapaciousness could

13

be symbolized by the wolf, etc., etc." Indication, symbol and image are wrought into one condensed statement which is artistic and which moves us because of the daring and the aptness of the condensation. It is, in fact, the very untruth to nature which makes its art, the horrible impossibility enlarges its descriptive force. Thus a truth of description may violate a truth of fact; indeed, in literature the utmost licence is permitted to the writer with facts of description. Everything may be subjected to the inner sensations of the writer. Nature is seen as mirrored in a temperament, and as the mood passes from placidity to agitation the semblance of nature becomes reflected as in a looking-glass of flexible material which can be twisted this way and that, giving a hundred distortions to the same object.

We are too liable to demand certain statements of fact from the painter, as though nature were a stable and positive certainty; whereas the nature which we conceive is in reality but the formation in our mind of the vision of previous generations of painters. I do not mean that without pictures nature would not be seen. Naturally nature is visible, but it is visible under certain preconceptions which prevent us from perceiving other facts. The invention of the photograph showed us certain facts of nature which had hitherto escaped observation. The fact which, perhaps, is the most noteworthy is that of the perspective of upright lines. We are, of course, well aware that horizontal lines going away from us run into perspective, and we have accepted this fact of vision as pictorial possibility, although the Chinese have not.* We must at the same time be aware that vertical lines are also subject to the same laws, and this the photograph shows clearly. But this law of nature we are disinclined to adopt as an artistic fact. We are aware also that all lines sufficiently long are subjected to this perspective effect, there being in fact only two lines in nature which are visibly straight, the lines passing vertically and horizontally through the centre of vision.

* Because, as will be shown later, converging lines cause suggestions of "movement" which would disturb the Chinese artist's theories of balance.

Thus, if we are facing a long building we get the following effect, the long lines curving in obedience to the laws of perspective :—

Since these facts of perspective are ignored in art, and since our eyes are not trained to look for them, we ignore them in nature, and, indeed, in spite of their existence, they are difficult to perceive. It is difficult to realize that when we are sitting in a room the walls visually slope inward, or that when we face a piece of architecture such as Hampton Court it is usually barrel shaped in outline. The steps of St. Paul's are built with a slight horizontal curve to defeat this phenomenon.

If we claim that the difference between the camera and our eye is that the camera has a fixed centre of vision, whereas we swing our vertical centre of sight as we turn round, we do not make nature any the more stable by our attempt to escape from error. As we swing about, each vertical line as we look at it becomes upright, the other lines going off into perspective, and so in fact all of them swing about in the most confusing way as we move our eyes—the Greeks, with the good taste that inspired their architecture, avoided all vertical straight lines in their best work.

Thus, we see that nature possesses facts which are incompatible with our natural idea of artistic licence. In addition to these, the defects of accurate observation by the eye are shown by a series of well-known diagrams known as optical illusions, by means of which parallel lines are made to appear not parallel, squares of the same size appear of different sizes and so on. These experiments show that " nature " is a tricky person to make definite statements about.

The first quarrel with the great public on the matter of art arose with the Impressionists. The little differences which arose previously, such as that with Corot—who was accused of giving cloud banks and columns of smoke instead of trees—and that with Millet, which was chiefly founded on amour-propre, never rose to a sufficient acerbity to include the general mass of the spectators. The critics attacked Delacroix, and accused him of giving them corpses instead of human flesh (what did they think of Crivelli or of Piero della Francesca ?), but the public passed by with, perhaps, a smiling shrug.

With the Impressionists, however, it became angry almost to madness. At the time of the Salon des Réfusés many a Frenchman would gladly have murdered Monet or Renoir. This was because these painters showed up a hitherto but half suspected fact of nature. The Old Masters had noted that a material in light appeared often different in colour from that of its shadows ; but they had, generally, so blended these colours that the colour of the material was never in doubt. They had gradually impressed on the public a fallacious notion of a burnt umber tree which was accepted with such faith that the green tree had to fight hard for admittance into art. When, however, a blue tree was presented to it, the public revolted. Yet, as a matter of fact, trees are often blue, and are very seldom burnt umber.

An object is of a colour because it reflects certain rays. A leaf is green because it reflects green, but if a leaf is placed in a red light, so that no green rays can be reflected, the leaf appears black. A leaf under a blue light will appear blue, because there are no yellow rays with which to make up green ; a shiny leaf will seem more blue than a dull leaf, because it is a better reflector. Under the intensely blue sky of Southern France it is possible to have such an excess of blue rays, that to the man who has divested his mind of the pre-conceived idea that trees *are* green (or burnt umber), the leaves of the tree reflect far more blue than green, and in fact appear blue. This does not, however, prevent the observer in question from perceiving that the tree is really green. Thus he is faced with a double path, only one of which can be followed. He can paint the tree green, or blue, as he wishes. But he cannot paint it so that one can see it as green or blue at will. As the Impressionists were making a study of the nature of light, they naturally painted the tree so that it was true to their point of view.

Thus we see that in colour nature has two incompatible truths as she had in perspective. A line can be, at once, straight by knowledge and curved by vision ; a colour can be green by knowledge and blue by vision.

But in the Impressionists we see not only a startling presentation of nature's facts, but also a startling method of presentation. The Renaissance and early Dutch painters had begun the analysis of nature as an analysis of fact. Their highest lyricism grows out of a lust for such things as perspective, anatomy, representation of surfaces and the exhibition of antique lore. This period comes to an end with Claude, Poussin, Velazquez and Chardin. Already Watteau foreshadows something quite different. The movement which begins with David and ends with Manet is in reality only an imitation on a smaller scale of what has gone before. It tries to delay the fatal moment. It researches over the old heap which has already been almost emptied of value, giving the search an interest new in material, but not new in analysis. However, this new interest forces the artists to a broader statement. Manet is a hasty Velazquez with a Japanese accent.

The analysis of nature as a tangible fact comes to an end about the moment when the philosophical doubt of nature as a tangible fact is becoming understood. The Impressionists' abrupt change, from the study of the tangible to the study of the intangible—light, is not too far removed from Kant's declaration that space is a property of the mind. I wish to make no claim that the Impressionists had any ideas of being practical philosophers ; but I do suggest that ideas become commonly suitable for the human race at certain stages of development, and that these ideas appear spontaneously under different aspects.

C

Painting leaves the study of nature as fact, and turns its attention to an analysis of the means by which nature is perceived. The Impressionists suddenly became aware of the fact that paint is not light ; and they had to devise means by which to key up the pitch of their pictures to the highest point in order to represent *effects* of light.

The fact that, on the whole, we tend to accept painting as a fairly faithful representation of fact can be made to illustrate in reality how far painting is from any actual *truth* to nature. Under *certain* circumstances only we can almost imitate the appearances of nature. Holbein's table is a well-known example ; another is that of the painted fly which the emperor tried to brush off his picture. As long as an object shows no reflections of actual light—such as the high sparkle on a glass bottle, or the glint in the eye—an object placed within doors can be copied with a fair accuracy. The light falls equally on picture and on object, the lightest white can be matched with white paint, and the darkest dark is not very appreciably darker than black. But, once a glint of reflected exterior light enters into the matter, the painter is lost. His highest white is much darker than this sparkle. Let us, for instance, imagine the glint on a white cup. If white paint is to represent the glint, then the actual colour of the cup must be represented as darker than white, since the glint is so much more brilliant than the white cup. This means that the whole picture has to be placed lower in brilliance than the reality, in order to give light enough to the glint. This fact of the powerlessness of paint to equal light led to the invention of that dark glass called the " Lorraine glass," which has the effect of lowering the value of a white cloud in the sky to the value of white paint on canvas, with the result that, when one gets to the shadowy parts of the picture, all the subtle changes of shadow which nature shows, are lost in the dark confusion which represents these parts in old pictures.

The Impressionists, seeking for a means to increase in their pictures the effects of luminosity which they were studying, found that by painting in spots of pure tint, placed side by side, or hatched together, instead of mixed, a richer colour was produced. They noted also that contrasts could be increased by using a colour with its complement—as blue against orange, red against green—and could be diminished by using similar colours against one another. Thus, the novel search on the part of the Impressionists forced upon them the recognition of a new process of painting as well as certain physical laws about the use of colour itself.

They further discovered that the best way in which to study the effects of light was by means of fleeting rapid glances, which summed up an impression of the object rather than made a detailed analysis. They found, indeed, that nature is a very unstable thing if considered from various aspects. They found that a shadow beneath a tree which might be bright violet at first glance would if long stared at quickly lose its colour, and in the end could be imagined almost any tint of greyish quality that one wished.

Although plain colours are fairly positive in character, there is a curious quality about subtle tints when observed in nature. This quality is especially aggravating to the student. At first glance one is certain of the tint, but a second examination makes one hesitate, a third leads one to doubt, and a prolonged final analysis plunges the student into despair. This is due to the fact that to the super-imposed colour texture of nature which we have already mentioned, a third is added; a colour may be influenced by the colours around it, and will tend to take on the complementary colour to the strongest opposing tint. Thus, a shadow tends to appear purple when under green trees. If, however, we stare at this shadow alone we lose the colour influence of the trees as contrast, but now get the double colour scheme of the local colour of the shadowed object and the reflections of green from the green trees above. I can assure the reader that these conflicting colour-schemes in nature often reduce the poor student to an agony of indecision of which he cannot discover the cause.

But to work out a broad view of nature's colour by means of fleeting glances, was not in reality *analysis* of nature. It was impossible to study details of form by fleeting glances, so details of form had to be rejected. The Impressionists, although they had the belief that they were still walking strongly in the tenets of " nature study," were in truth setting out on a very different road. If we chose to consider nature, as she is generally considered, as something external to ourselves and tangible, the Impressionists open the door to a study of reactions between ourselves and nature which had hitherto been unsuspected. It may be noted that as man becomes less and less a necessary object in painting—until the moment arrives when he can be omitted altogether from a landscape —by so much the more is the personality of the artist demanded visibly in the work.

The Impressionists open the way to a study, not of what man *sees in* nature, but of *how* nature affects man. As in every other form of human development, we pass from legend to observation, from observation to question, from question to explanation. This is a mere advance in knowledge, not in beauty. We cannot say that the legend of Horus or of Apollo is more or less beautiful than the fact of the revolution of the planets ; beauty does not depend upon developed knowledge. So there is no claim that the art of question is more beautiful than the art of observation. (The subject of beauty itself must be left for a later page.) The beauty produced by any particular development of art depends solely on the power of the artist and upon nothing else. Michael Angelo, Rubens or Rembrandt could have worked in any way they liked. The beauty produced depends only on the *man*, not on his methods. The methods themselves are settled by external fate. The developments of modern art which we are about to study have developed inexorably. One has no more reason to condemn them than a flat-earth faddist has to condemn our earth's unfortunate rotundity. Picasso is but a cog in the wheel of time.

The turns of opinion concerning the Impressionists have more or less settled in swing to-day, and I doubt if any of the artists who composed the Impressionist group proper can be called really great ;

just as no really great men are associated with the invention of the steam engine.   Both of these movements were inevitable and came about by the intermediary of men of high intelligence and of moderate genius.   At the first exhibition of Impressionism there were about a hundred exhibitors.   How many of these are to-day known to the public ?   The three most famous were never *au fond* Impressionists. These three, Renoir, Degas and Cézanne are all in direct contradiction with one of the chief tenets of the Impressionist theory— that of taking the subject direct from nature without any artistic control or composition of the pictorial elements.   Of the other painters Monet, Sisley, Guillemin and Pissarro had high talent. Of these seven men, the first three would have made their mark in any age and under any conditions.   The last four are gifted, but their names still enjoy undue prominence owing to the novelty of their research and the new technique which was inspired by it.

Leaving Renoir and Cézanne for future consideration, we may now follow out the direct development of the ideas inherent in Impressionism.   These ideas, though disguised under the aspect of a study of nature, were in reality the beginning of the study of nature's effect upon man.   The methods of the Impressionists first hinted at by Watteau, developed by Constable, Turner and Delacroix, gradually banished from the palette all the earthly colours, in order to get some hint of the brilliance of light.   The Impressionists used only the brightest colours, producing their secondaries, purples, olives, greens and so on by mixture.   But this process of mixing entails some loss of brilliance.   If we mix a bright yellow with a pure blue the green resulting is not the mean of brilliance between the intensities of the two colours, but is considerably darker than this mean.   There is, however, a method of producing a green which is approximately the true mean between the two colours, and is therefore considerably brighter than the mixed colour.

If we examine a plate taken by the Lumiere process of colour photography, we shall see that all the varied colours are made up in reality with three pure colours only, and that these three pure colours in microscopic dots make up all the other colours. The spots are so small that the eye cannot distinguish them separately; and they blend to form the various colours in the photograph. If we magnify a picture of this plate on to a screen with a magic lantern, we will find that, though at a distance the picture seems as precise as before, if we come closer we can perceive the dots of colour of which it is made up. That is to say, juxtaposed dots of various colours, if sufficiently small, blend optically into a single colour of the same tint that the colours would make if mixed. But the resultant colour, being an optical mixture and not a mechanical one, does not lose brilliance in the process, and your yellow and blue so blended would form a green more brilliant than that produced by mixture. So that if a picture is painted in spots of pure colour, it will be more brilliant than a picture produced by any other means. This discovery, a natural product of the efforts of the Impressionists, was made by Paul Signac, then a young disciple of the Impressionist movement. Until his death Monsieur Signac was the President of the Société des Indépendants. This discovery must be ranked as an interesting scientific theory of the properties of pigment.

But a second figure associates itself with Signac to form the school of Neo-Impressionist (this group must not be confounded with the Post-Impressionist). Another name by which this school is known is that of Pointillist—from their habit of painting in small spots—which perhaps distinguishes the school better from the more general title which is used to cover the whole of the modern æsthetic developments. This man was Seurat. He was a student of Beaux Arts, but even as a student he went his own way, refusing to accept the authority of the academicians. He was a man of intensely analytical mind, spending as many days in the Louvre as in the Academy, always demanding " Why ? " whereas others were content to ask " How ? " He made a scientific analysis of the line, composition, chiaroscuro and colour of the Old Masters, of the Orientals, and of the painters of his day. Gradually he worked out a theory

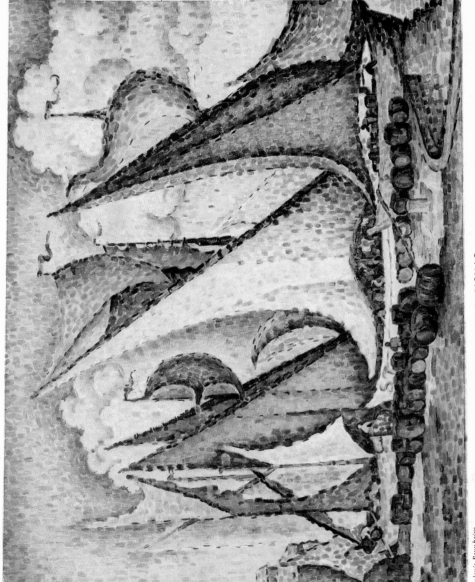

PAUL SIGNAC

MEDITERRANEAN SAILING BOATS

of rhythm of composition and contrast of colour, and later on a theory of colour itself. Then he met Signac and adopted the technical methods of Signac, while Signac learned the scientific theories of composition from Seurat. Seurat died young, having produced three or four canvases of great brilliance and beauty.*

The Pointillists, working on Seurat's and Signac's ideas, tried to give to their practice a completeness of theory which is not quite warranted. It is possible after the masterpiece has been created to work out the structure upon which it was built, but to invent rules for the creation of masterpieces is a futile pursuit. The masterpiece is the result of the man ; the great artist can break all the rules and produce great art, the mere painter can follow all the rules and produce nothing. However, rules which show a conscious attitude towards the art practised usually indicate a general activity of mind from which nothing but good can come. We must not quarrel with Leonardo da Vinci, nor with Goethe or Stephenson for trying to penetrate the secrets of their crafts. Signac has given us himself a summary of the Pointillist finger-posts to art in his book, *From Delacroix to Neo-Impressionism* :

" Guided by tradition and by science he (the Neo-Impressionist) will harmonize the composition of his idea ; that is to say, he will adapt the lines (directions and angles), the chiaroscuro (tones), the colours (tints) to the character on which he wishes pictorially to insist. Lines will in general become horizontal if calmness is desired, ascending if joy, descending if sorrow is demanded. The intermediate lines will determine other sensations in infinite variety. A play of colour not less expressive and varied is related to this lineal interplay : warm colours and high-pitched tones correspond to ascending lines, cold colour and deep tones should predominate in descending compositions : and calm horizontal lines will be intensified by an equilibrium more or less complete of warm and cold colours, of clear and intense tones. Subjecting thus colour and line to the emotion which he feels and which he wishes to convey, the painter will be doing the work of a true poet, of a true creator."

* One of Seurat's best pictures, " The Chahut," seems to have been directly inspired by a frieze of Egyptian dancers executed 2500 B.C.

It will be seen that here is a great development from the Impressionist idea of painting. In theory the Impressionists confined themselves entirely to nature, disdaining composition, striving to catch nature unawares. *Ils peignent comme l'oiseau chante.* Their intensification of colour was but the strivings of paint to *rival* the brilliance of light.

But the Neo-Impressionists have become conscious of the physiological effects of colour and of line on human emotions. They are no longer men darting out to catch butterfly beauty on the wing, they are the men who have kept beauty captive in their minds till an egg is produced, and from this they desire to breed other beauties. But the rule still holds that out of some thousands of eggs which the butterfly lays only one may come to maturity.

There are usually two classes of people (I speak, of course, of those interested in art matters) of which one class loves to understand consciously and persuades itself that beauty is increased by understanding ; the other class on the other hand has a horror of perceiving any of the mechanisms by which art is produced. Both classes are wrong. Beauty is not increased by understanding, because at its root beauty is a reaction of the senses. It is possible that through understanding the path to beauty is made more easy, but understanding tends to formulate rules : rules create preconceived ideas. Such people are apt to remember the wonderful construction of the clock and to forget that it is intended to tell the time. They may lose the true sense of beauty in the magic of a comprehension of how beauty is created. The other class relies on its sensibility alone, and is in fear that, by understanding, the delicate balance of this sensibility may be disturbed. Like the dog in Æsop's fable, they fear to lose a substance in grasping for a shadow. This is a fear due to a misplaced sense of romance. They are like a savage who could believe the clock as a time-telling instrument if he imagined the hands to be controlled by some genie whose heart-beat was the ticking of the pendulum, but who would mistrust it if he were made aware that it was but mere self-regulating mechanism.

SEURAT
STUDY FOR THE MODELS

To understand that a painter does not copy nature, but that he imposes on to nature a design wrought from his own brain, to learn how this design is constructed and to perceive its qualities and effects, to perceive how the painter may reveal a new aspect of sensibility in response to his deliberately (or instinctively) ordered schemes, does not invalidate the beauty he creates. It but intensifies the mystery which surrounds human consciousness. It makes us aware of a magic hitherto unexpected.

There is a danger that knowledge may lead to pedantry. Our professors and savants are terrible examples. If ever we begin to set knowledge up in the place of emotional reaction, if we make knowledge the master instead of the servant, the knowledge becomes a curse.

Young Beethoven's music master said to him : " Your exercise is wrong, you have used consecutive fifths, which are forbidden by the rules of music." Beethoven replied : " They now are right. *I* have authorized them."

The true use of knowledge is to deepen our sense of the marvellous, no revelation can do anything more than increase our sense of wonder.

The self-conscious seekings of the Neo-Impressionist (Pointillist) group do not indicate that art grows necessarily more beautiful thereby. It is a truism that art does not grow more beautiful by increase of knowledge. Neither the learning of Leonardo nor of Sir Joshua Reynolds helped either to be a better artist than was Botticelli or Gainsborough respectively. But this growth of self-consciousness does show one thing. It shows that art has not degenerated into a stagnant state of self-content. It shows that art is elastic enough to keep pace with the mental growth of the civilization : Art, by developing, proves that it is still alive, that by growing it is, indeed, in the exact contrary state to that which it has been accused of, namely, decadence. Art falls into decadence when it stagnates. Bouguereau and Poynter are the decadents, not Cézanne or Van Gogh. It is not new movement which we must fear, but lack of movement, or rather a lack of movement commensurate with its period. The arts of Egypt or of China, which represent societies stable over centuries, could show a stability parallel to that of their social frame. The arts of Greece grew and declined within a short period.

The intellectual development of art which starts with Cézanne and the Pointillists is a necessary stage through which art has to pass. The fact that Cézanne was a great artist, and that Seurat was highly gifted, has in reality nothing to do with the techniques to which they gave birth. Theories are necessary developments of a social condition ; the artists are but haphazard personalities in whom nature has contrived to unite a fortunate combination of qualities. But as one of these qualities is a super-sensitiveness to the social conditions of his time, it is usually found that the great artist, in his quick response to the conditions, is almost always ahead of the more sluggish mass which makes up the general public. From this fact comes the frequent tension between public and artist, and the consequent lack of public appreciation of his day from which so many great artists have suffered.

CHAPTER III

CÉZANNE

realism
suggestion

IN the Luxembourg gallery are two small pictures by Cézanne; neither one nor the other a very pronounced example of him at his best. One is a picture of a sea with distant hills very boldly suggested and might for a moment catch the eye of the casual visitor; the other is a study taken in a farm-yard, and is so blatantly lacking in picturesque subject-matter that the average gallery tourist would never become aware of its existence. If the picture did catch his eye he might halt for a moment amazed : " I wonder why the fellow painted that," he would muse, " I expect he was afraid it was going to rain, and just kept his hand in doing a corner of the cow-shed." The picture represents a piece of low, uninteresting building seen between two yard walls, one in light, the other in shadow. The light wall seems merely a bar of white paint from top to bottom of one side of the frame, thus appearing merely to cut off about a fifth of the picture space. The floor of the yard is green rough grass, and over the roof of the shed shows an uninteresting piece of hill with a few trees upon it. A dead tree stands in the yard, and another on the hill-side carries the line of this tree farther up into the canvas. A small, dull, roughly painted canvas, holding nothing apparently remarkable save for the ugly and useless white strip of wall, which seems to do nothing except to reduce the width of the *picture* by about a fifth part.

I am quite ready to confess that when I came first to Paris, with my eyes veiled by prejudice, for a full year I never perceived this canvas in spite of frequent visits to the Luxembourg gallery. When I did notice it I marvelled, not at its beauty, but at its dullness.

27

The white wall, above all, offended me. " One *cannot* compose pictures like that," I said to myself. I do not remember now how many years it needed to awaken my appreciation, but gradually the picture acquired a subtle interest. I tired of the Simons, the Menards; Monet and Pissarro began to lose their flavour. This picture, on the contrary, along with some of the Renoir's, seemed to grow more worth while with every visit. Now, I cannot imagine how I ever found it dull, for, in spite of the fact that it is hardly a masterpiece of Cézanne's, there is a magic in it. I am ready to acknowledge that I have heartily hated almost every one of the artists I am now writing about, at any rate as far as Picasso. My enthusiasms have been come at slowly. There is nothing that an opponent of the Post-Cézanne developments can feel *against* these pictures that I have not felt myself once—to-day I feel otherwise. I have come to this point by the pursuit of my own art. As I came in face with problems which I had to solve, I found that others had already solved them. But I could not perceive this solution until I myself had worked out the problem. This was possibly because I did not attack the problem in a sufficiently humble spirit. There is, indeed, little humility in mankind's attitude towards art. Everybody knows what art is ; or rather everybody can affirm what is not " art." Prejudice is the worst hanging judge in history.

I do not wish to assert that I have been in succession an imitator of Cézanne, Van Gogh, Matisse or Picasso ; for I have struggled after things of my own feelings. But I have found that problems which have stood in my way as unperceived stumbling-blocks have been solved, each in its way, by the artists named above, and I have gradually become aware of certain basic ideas of art which seem to lie beneath all manifestations of art worthy of consideration, and I have realized that when these qualities are present a peculiar kind of pleasure is given, whereas it is lacking when these qualities are absent.

Since I originally ignored this Cézanne farm-yard because of the dullness of its subject-matter, it may be rather interesting to follow out the development of subject-matter in European art.

Literature begins solely as autobiography, but, since painting can hardly become autobiographical before the invention of the looking-glass—so beloved by egoistic painters—the painter begins on his fellow man. Accessories or animals are only added when necessary. Pieces of canopies over the Virgin's heads gradually widen into churches, and by degrees a perception of nature grows. In the time of Reynolds, however, landscape even accompanied by man was considered a second-rate art. Finally the landscape was admitted as a subject unaccompanied by man, but the landscape had to have some mood, by which to excite emotion. It had to be sentimental, as in Corot, or dramatic, as in Turner. To be exact, no matter what was painted one had to be able to get from the picture some *picturesque* sentiment. Still lives, for instance, had to be floral or edible in nature, landscapes had to soothe the weary spirit by suggestions of repose and peace, or allow the vision to escape over broad vistas ; figure painting naturally is interesting in all its phases to egoistic man. Even the Impressionists gave the glory and warmth of sunlight—I was then at this point.

But this ordinary little corner of a farm-yard had none of these things, and the white fifth part of the canvas seemed a deliberate offence against ideas of picture-making.

Thus the landscapes of the Pre-Impressionist days had to charm the spectator, because the object itself in nature would have charmed him. The picture, thus, was to some extent used as a stimulant to the recollection of remembered pleasures. The objections to Millet's work were that he painted unpleasant subjects, that peasants were not beautiful people to contemplate. To-day we realize that Millet was creating a new kind of sentimental beauty of subject-matter, a beauty which in time almost obliterated all feeling for the ideal beauty of the academical school of his day, and gave rise to a new academical ideal of beauty of subject-matter which produced Dagnan-Bouveret, Cottet, Simon, as well as the countless hosts of Breton *croûtes* which still cumber the Salon exhibition.

The majority of pictures please because they stimulate a

recollection of remembered pleasures. The artist, as well as educating the eye, has educated the range of objects in which contemplation can find pleasure. Thus Millet added " the peasant " as an object fitted to be admired. But the public mistakes the artist's aim. He is in reality trying to make a clear division between two conceptions of beauty. These two conceptions are often jarring, and while the artist may perceive one aspect the public is still only realizing the other. Pictorial beauty is a question of the eye alone, but senti-mental ideas may conceive a thing as unpleasant and from these conceptions it will be considered to be pictorially ugly. Let us take an instance.

Corrugated iron is a building material detested by country gentlefolk. It carries a reflection of the manufactory into the tran-quillity of the landscape. Its reasons for existing are purely com-mercial—it is cheap and easy to erect—therefore it imposes a jarring note into the idyllic scenery of some agrarian locality. It is con-sidered ugly. But corrugated iron is not an ugly substance. It has a fine blue tint which echoes our pale skies and the buildings made of it are unpretentious tent-like structures, or else introduce fine curved effects into the " cubism " of our country farm-yards. At a distance of a mile it would be impossible to distinguish optically between a small corrugated iron building and a tent of blue canvas. Yet the former would be dubbed hideous, the latter charming. Thus, the ugliness of corrugated iron is not a true visual ugliness, but due to a mental conception of corrugated iron as a material; however, in ordinary conversation only the *visual* properties of corrugated iron are mentioned. The same is true of the frog. The frog is considered ugly because it is cold and clammy and faintly caricatures humanity. Yet the Japanese artist can show with his swift brush that the frog is in truth *visually* beautiful.

The tendency with humanity has been to accept with reluctance the various revelations of beauty, but to accept these nevertheless. But it accepts them in such a way that it ends by blunting the very point which the artist was striving to sharpen. Thus, when the artist has shown that there is beauty to be found in the peasant, the public accepts the peasant as pictorially beautiful. From this it follows (for the public) that *any* picture of *any* peasant is a beautiful picture. In time any picture of factories or corrugated iron will be considered beautiful pictures, because factories have just been admitted as beautiful subject-matter, and corrugated iron will be allowed very shortly.

But the artist of to-day is not trying to add little by little to the list of objects which can be allowed fit matter as beauty " containers." He is trying to state clearly that beauty lies in *everything*, that from his point of view beauty has nothing to do with mental conceptions which have been formed by the aid of the other senses. He is trying to free the eye from the prejudices imposed upon it by things learned and things heard. He is trying to destroy the illusion of the *picturesque*, and to build up in its place a sentiment for the pictorial.

It is usually considered that the *picturesque* is the fittest material for picture making : the ruined cottage, the old peasant woman, the blasted oak and so on form the staple subject-matter of second-rate painters. But the truth is that the picturesque is that group of subject-matter which has up to now received artistic sanction *in detail ;* and arouses sentimental emotion not because it is necessarily beautiful, but because it has become associated with dogmas or preconceptions of the beautiful. Indeed, the picturesque is the most dangerous of subject-matter, because this subject-matter contains sentimental associations of beauty which tend to veil by means of this sentiment any shortcomings from real plastic beauty.

Cézanne is almost the first painter who dared to eschew all suggestions of the picturesque. Many of his pictures are about as picturesque as a back yard. Yet one does not get tired of them. Once one lets oneself become aware of the particular kind of beauty which he is striving after, it does not pall as do picturesque beauties, but grows in force. We derive a new pleasure, not the resurrection of a past enjoyment. And, if one allows oneself to be drawn along this road, one will find that one's appreciation of all painting is deepening and growing broader. One can assert that the person who cannot perceive the beauties of Cézanne has never properly seen the beauties of the Old Masters. By understanding Cézanne all good painting seems to become more significant; and all bad painting less valuable.

This farm-yard in the Luxembourg is a characteristic example of Cézanne's outlook. It has all the virtues and no graces. The colours are admirably harmonized, with just that hint of the unexpected which is necessary in truly admirable colour; if the eye is allowed consciously to follow the lines of the picture one finds a careful, pleasing, rhythmical swing which is as joyous as the movement of the sea. If one regards one after another the simple spaces into which the picture is divided one finds that they all—the flat ground, the two walls, the cattle shed, the rounded hill, the sky—seem to be united in a subtle relationship of shapes, sizes, and sensations of depth (or recession) which gives an increasing pleasure the more poignantly they are perceived. The white wall conveys the sensation of being shut in within a limited space.

None of these qualities are qualities derived from imitating or from copying nature, none of them have any relationship with the picturesque. These belong to the basic virtues of painting which spring from the brain of the artist alone. Nature is indeed a haphazard millionaire flinging together good and bad: but the beauties in this picture are beauties conceived by the mind. A musician may perceive in a few notes of bird song the suggestion for a melody. He completes it from his imagination. The painter may perceive in nature the suggestion for a picture. He, too, completes it from his imagination.

This attitude of the artist towards his art makes a complete revolution of the art of drawing. It has been generally imagined that good drawing consists in an accurate representation of the appearance of nature, that drawing was in fact an amplification of the statement that "facts are stubborn things." It has been taken

PAUL CEZANNE
THE SMOKER

for granted that the artists of other countries, such as Egypt or China, did not draw well because they could not, because, in fact, drawing was too difficult for them.   Yet is it not absurd to suppose that the Chinese artist who could draw with precision the fearful intricacies of a chrysanthemum could not have drawn the simple problem of a face, or hand, had he wished to do so?   There is many an artist alive to-day who can draw a face with perfect accuracy who cannot draw a chrysanthemum.   Yes; the accurate drawing of fact is not indeed a very difficult matter.

Cézanne's idea of drawing is based upon a standard more difficult for the public to judge than mere accuracy.   It is based upon the idea that the artist's first and most important task is to create this sensation of rhythmical movement of lines and ordered sensations of depth.   Cézanne's drawing is not a drawing of outline, it is a drawing of space.   He is not trying to get an accurate imitation, for that was not sufficiently interesting for him.   He is trying to blend a drawing of space sensations with a rhythmical pattern—which has been called " Arabesque."

A still life by Cézanne is not as the older still lives were, a collection of suitable objects which have been arranged till they form a tasteful group.   Every object in a Cézanne composition has its purpose, and is painted to give the eye just its proper amount of interest and no more.   Every object is considered not for itself, but on account of its relative value in the picture.   This had been done in former times for tone.   That is, the values of colour had been carefully worked out as relative attractions of dark and light, for all Old Masters depend to a large extent upon this property.   Thus, if one of the Old Masters found that a white spot in a picture was disturbing to the general pattern, he darkened it down until it took its place *as pattern*.   But such a discipline had not been used for drawing by Europeans.   Cézanne did it.

In the average " correct " drawing, which can be found by the hundred in the studios of Chelsea, there is no sense whatever of the relative drawing of objects.   Every object drawn is considered as a

D

thing by itself, and the nearer the precision approaches that of a mechanically plotted delineation, the better the drawing is presumed to be. But is it certain that we *see* things with such accuracy? We do not. One must never forget that optical illusion of the two lines crossed by diagonal lines, which is so well known and so baffling. If these cross lines cause so much optical disturbance that lines measurably parallel appear no longer parallel, what is the more subtle interaction of lines in nature? Thus, while we know that the opening of a cup is an ellipse, do we actually see an ellipse? In fact, we perceive the ellipse with very little accuracy.

With the relative importance of objects in the composition enters another factor in the consideration of drawing. If one draws a pattern in Arabesque one will find that any complete symmetrical figure—such as a perfect ellipse—will attract the eye so strongly that it tends to detach itself from the general pattern, to form an object apart. Thus, it may destroy the unity of the pattern. By thrusting itself so much upon the attention it interferes with the value of other more subtle rhythmical balances of pattern. The same is true of any symmetrical object, and also of perpendicular or of horizontal lines. Such forms all tend to disturb a general pattern, and must be used carefully and sparingly.

To Cézanne the rhythmical arrangements and the spatial qualities were all important; and he was aware that the accurate vision of nature is summary and conventional—rather than absolute. Therefore he does not hesitate to sacrifice the latter to the former. Whenever he has to choose between the academic idea of drawing or his own idea of space composition and rhythmical design, he always sacrifices the former. He will make the two sides of a bottle different in shape, he will cause the bottle to slope at an angle instead of standing upright, he will distort a bowl from the ellipse, if these alterations improve his " drawing "; that is, his complete picture. When, however, he wishes to use a vertical line or a perfect ellipse, nobody is a more " accurate " draughtsman.

Cézanne himself has summed up the nature of his art in the

word to " realize." He is trying not merely to reproduce nature, but to present a nature more completely understood than had hitherto been presented. This fierce, never satisfied desire provided the driving force which comes out in his work as vitality.

Cézanne is primarily a realist. He begins with Courbet and Manet, touches Delacroix, becomes one of the Impressionist movement ; but none of these satisfied him. He wished to make from Impressionism something more solid. The Impressionists produced the effect of a momentary look at nature, they analysed the *effect* of light ; and at the first glance their pictures are satisfactory. But the pleasure does not last. Because they are swimming in light everything else is lost, objects in their pictures have no reality, they are tinted air, space is sacrificed, design often neglected. They reduce everything down to the first fact of vision, to pleasure in colour, they create colour harmonies out of reflected light and colour induction ; local colour is neglected because it interferes with their purpose. Because they created colour harmonies, and in so far as their artistic instincts have made them choose subjects which contained design—though conscious design was against their creed— the Impressionists were true artists. Monet paints a haystack several times from the same spot beneath varying aspects of light ; he was indifferent to the haystack, it was only the object which caught and reflected the illumination. But this analysis of superficial appearance was not enough for Cézanne. Beneath all these changes there is a reality—or to us there seems to be a reality—this reality is unchangeable. We admit this reality in the outline. We become philosophers with the outline separating the most poignant part of reality from appearance. Cézanne does not hesitate to outline with blue or with black in order to insist when necessary upon the logical reality of any object in his canvas. Always Cézanne is seeking to make this reality more tangible through the eyes.

We must admit that on the whole we attach ourselves to the " look of things," and we learn this " look " from the way in which others have represented it. The appearance which Cézanne presents is often different from the appearance to which we are accustomed because his sense of values is different. Cézanne strives to drive down to a reality which can only be felt and which seems to lie behind appearance. To attain this he tried to banish from his memory what he had learned from others. Instinctively he realized how much the eye trains itself from pictures. He tried to " change his eye." He says : " Perhaps we all paint by conventions, we must come to see the *real colours*. To do this we must forget what has been already done, and observe nature ; do everything from nature ; then, by clearing from our sight the vision of our predecessors, we shall perceive a world of new chromatic value." This is the root of his method. To carry out this idea, he looked at his subject far longer than he worked upon the canvas.

But, as I have pointed out, pure appearance of nature is extremely unstable. The longer one looks the more vacillating it becomes. Cézanne's method did give him a new eye, it enabled him to clear from his mind much of the conscious influence of his predecessors, but this weight of responsibility placed upon vision did not permit him to *see* nature more *absolutely* than other artists have seen her, for vision is relative, and absolute vision of nature impossible. The fact that the appearance of nature is unstable, combined with his slow thoughtful vision and his rejection of clichés in painting, enabled him to exercise upon his eye a self-hypnosis. He finally perceives in nature the colour which he feels to be right and which he puts down with precision and accuracy. The unconscious influence which he exercised over his vision was regulated by two factors, first his instinct for colour harmony, secondly his discovery of the spatial value of colour. The colour instinct makes him realize the inter-reactions of colours upon one another, and makes him—perhaps in spite of his intention—cling to the principle enunciated by Delacroix, but used previously by Constable and also by Watteau, that " a colour space is more rich if not laid on in one tint, but composed of many variations and gradations of the same colour." The second discovery of the spatial value of colours—

Louvre

CÉZANNE

HOUSES IN A LANDSCAPE. (WATER-COLOUR)

that yellows tend to come forward, that blues and violets appear to recede, in a canvas—by means of which the space sensations of a picture could be powerfully increased, undoubtedly influences Cézanne not only in his choice of subject, but also in his vision of colour. It is impossible to imitate Nature's colour effects in paint. Cézanne knew this, and thus when he speaks of clearing his eye it is not for the purpose of more closely imitating nature, but in order to find ways of translating her into plastic art, ways which had not been previously explored and which might give results more positive than those of his predecessors.

The highest emotional value which Nature possesses is its spatial value. When we perceive this positively all other beauties tend to diminish in value, we do not realize the contour of the hills when the beauty of a broad vista bursts upon us, but the space. Space takes us in the throat and shakes us with emotion. In the cathedral, space first moves us and on it our final remembrance lingers. Cézanne, striving to realize nature, struggles with the problem of space. The spatial value of colouring forces itself upon him, and in consequence of his solution of this problem he forces upon the spectator a realization of space which is far more poignant than our normal sensations.

In order to create these two values, the reality of objects—in opposition to mere appearance—and the quality of space, Cézanne, breaking away entirely from the Impressionists, to a large extent casts out light and shade from his pictures. Or rather we may say that he forgoes *effects* of light. He uses light only to bring about more positive reality or more clear definition of shape, and when the light effect threatens to destroy his reality, as light effects so often tend to do, he ignores or bends the light effect to his own purpose.

It must be remembered that an effect of light is the most fugitive of phenomena, and that the concentration upon these effects which is so marked a phase of a certain section of contemporary artists is of a sentimental rather than of an æsthetic nature. They strive to awaken in the spectator a reflection of the joy he feels upon a summer day, they try to borrow from the joy of nature some analogous joy which association will attach to the picture.

But, though Cézanne's art in appearance seems to depart widely from the conventional vision of his day, it is only a surface difference. The art of Cézanne is a direct descendant of the French tradition of painting. He himself says, "We must remake Poussin from nature." He clings to the French tradition only for what was good in it, and what was good in the French tradition is that which is good in all arts.

But he realized also that, though he was in the direct line of the French classical tradition, yet he had brought something new into it. The life of a school of painting is very like any other example of life. It has its youth, its maturity, its senility. But a tradition may be likened rather to a family. It has succeeding members, each of whom bears a family resemblance to the others, yet with a distinct personality. The school dies in senility, but the descendant, though differing in appearance from the father, carries on the strain. Yet the new school must in turn pass through its life processes. Cézanne, however, while asserting his descendance through the French classic ideals, foresees that his contributions to art must have a great effect once they have been understood. He said, "I am the primitive of a method I have invented."

CHAPTER IV

VINCENT VAN GOGH

ONE might ask : " If our *vision* of nature is modified by art, surely it cannot matter whether nature can be imitated or no : if the artist can give us in a painting something which we can recognize as nature, surely, then, the beauty of nature should tell as strongly in the painting as any beauty that the artist can create by means of this complicated brain work of organization ? "

It is widely assumed that the highest beauties of pictorial art are less poignant than the most moving beauties of nature. Before some impressive prospect the tourist continually is exclaiming : " Ah, no artist could paint this." The tourist is right. That " Nature imitates Art " is not an exact truth : the phrase would be better put, " Our memory of nature imitates art." When we wish to compare nature with some new phase of art, the evidence we bring is not that of what we have truly seen in nature, because this vision is too subtle, too fugitive, too complex to be called up. We bring a generalized memory composed of artistic commonplaces, as near to truth as is the newspaper serial writer's description of a love scene. When we are actually face to face with nature the beauty which moves us is dependent upon a feeling of more or less exact proportions between the different objects in the scene. Say that we are gazing at an effect of fading daylight over a broad vista. The precise quality of the faint distant hills against the sky, the subtle changes as ridge after ridge swells nearer to us, the play of colour and of light over the foreground, distinctive patterns formed by rifts of shadow, the stereoscopic power of the eyes, and the selective power

39

of the comprehension, each plays a part like the separate dancers in a ballet. When one tries to copy this in paint, one must at once begin to make compromises. White paint is not as light as the sky by ten degrees, black paint is not as black as the deepest shadow by the same amount. Therefore between white paint and black paint the artist must reduce the real contrasts by proportionate amounts, and in nature every exact change of shade will be ten times more powerful than the painter can afford to make it in paint. Although the memory cannot apprehend that the painting is everywhere a weakened version of the original, yet the instinctive sense says that something is lacking. With every one of these compromises something has faded from the depicted version of the scene. It is as though the ballet had been copied by actors who made flaccid and petty in the place of active and full gestures.

The Chinese or Japanese painter does not attempt this compromise. He knows that one of the factors which produces æsthetic emotion is the graduated contrasts of the hills one against the other. He uses the white of his paper as sky, then places the correct contrast of the ridge of the farthest hill. Then, in order to get sufficient luminosity to place correctly the contrast of his next hill, he fades the farthest hill rapidly into white paper again. Thus, each hill-side fades at its foot into whiteness in order to provide sufficient range to produce his correct contrasts. He thus sacrifices an obvious fact of nature, to gain a subtler fact of æsthetic observation. Thus a daring artistic lie may contain more truth than an apparently truthful statement which is in fact a series of compromises—or, undetected understatements.

The artist who is merely imitator leaves to the spectator the task of creating for himself a beauty from the picture. The tendency is to substitute a memory for reality : to look upon a painting not as so much *actual and unique* beauty, but to use it as a means by which to recall the flavours of beauties previously enjoyed. The picture of the wide prospect puts us into the emotional state aroused by wide prospects in general, or may recall to us some beloved prospect in particular : a painting of a summer day on the river with a girl and pink sunshade awakens memories of moments of similar sweetness. Thus, the picture in reality but arouses a chain of associations, and it is the latter which stir us more than does the picture. In the painting which arouses no such associations, we fail to see beauty. The still life of two lemons and a cup leaves us cold. But, if somebody has vivid associations of lemons and cups, then this picture will have on him as powerful an effect as the river-girl and her parasol.

But if the artist can force into you a realization that *he* felt something extraordinary about the two lemons and the cup, then—no matter how he does it—he has created a true work of art, he is giving you something outside of your own emotional gamut. And art of this kind not only can rival nature, but can overtop it in beauty.

Cézanne does not descend into the particular. He is a lofty spirit to whom wide prospects, river girls, or lemons are usually similar, they are different examples of form existing in space out of which varied emotional matter can be produced. He paints his wife with the same emotional clarity as he paints a dish of apples ; he prefers a bunch of paper flowers to real ones because they last longer and can therefore be studied without disturbing haste. He laughed at Zola's description of him in *L'Œuvre*. " One does not commit suicide because a picture does not succeed," he remarked, " one pitches it out of the window and begins another." He practised as he preached. He used to leave his pictures in the fields, and the trees outside of his house often contained canvases which he had hurled out through the window.

But Vincent Van Gogh, the second of the artists most prominently connected with the modern developments of art, was the antithesis of Cézanne. Cézanne is a realist, he is trying to get behind appearance, to realize nature as something external to himself : Van Gogh is trying to reveal himself. Cézanne tries to perceive a " *world* of new chromatic value " ; Van Gogh evolves new chromatic values to explain what the world of ordinary chromatic values means to him, personally. Cézanne is always talking of Classicism, of Poussin, *après la nature*, of methods, " Everything in nature is modelled on the lines of the cube, the cone and the cylinder. If you understand how to paint these simple forms you can paint anything "; Van Gogh, on the other hand, talking of the Japanese, of plaguing himself by too much study of nature, elevating the imagination in contrast to the realistic, says : " I do not mean that I never turn my back boldly on nature . . . but I am frightened to death of losing accuracy of form. Perhaps later after ten years' study I shall try ; but really and truly I am so devoured by curiosity for the possible and actual that I have neither the wish nor the courage to seek an ideal which could arise out of my abstract studies."

Art has been defined as " nature seen through a temperament." The definition is no definition at all. Everybody sees nature through a temperament, each one sees it according to the education, development and personality of his perceptive powers. But there are two ways of accepting this temperamental veil which our senses cast over our vision. One may try to reduce the temperamental part to its lowest point, as the scientific observer has to do ; or one may submit oneself to the temperament in order to receive the most exhilarating visions which nature can give. No prophet has ever arisen with the former temperament. The greatest reformers or teachers have been moved not by a vision of man as he is, but of man as he might be. Cézanne is trying to create a world which is as real in its way as the world of perception, but a world ordered into a harmony of ideal form : Van Gogh, on the other hand, is trying to create a world more real than the world of perception. Both of these men exhibit the new spirit which was creeping into art. They realized *what* they were doing. Neither the one nor the other would have wished, like Corot, to go on playing his little melodies.

Van Gogh is clearly exhibited in his letters.* " I have painted seven studies of corn ; *quite against my will they are only landscapes.*

* *Letters of a Post-Impressionist* Translated with a preface by Anthony Ludovichi.

VAN GOGH
THE CYPRESS TREES

They are all of a yellow tone and were executed at a frantic speed, just as the reaper works silently in the sweltering sun with only one thought in his mind—to cut down as much as possible." The words which I put into italics give the gist of Van Gogh. To paint something which was only a landscape was not enough for him. He was once an evangelist in the Belgian coal mines, and he would wish his pictures to preach for him. They were to preach a more sensitive reaction to nature and to beauty than had hitherto been felt. He is one of the sons of God who must shout in the morning, and he wants us all to go out and shout with him. It is not unnatural that the normal part of the human race which has been drilled from babyhood to the sober-mindedness suitable for factory or office work is shocked at Van Gogh's passionate delirium of his vision of nature.

" Quite against my will they are only landscapes." Here is a text for a sermon on the spirit of adventure. Ruskin says : " All the pure and noble arts of peace are founded on war." He is preaching the dogmas of the futurists. But it is an untruth, the cause of art lies deeper than mere war. Art arises out of vitality, vitality in the past has forced men to war. The arts of China have not arisen from war, nor have those of Egypt. Art arises from the spirit of adventure latent in man ; that it so often is forced to find satisfaction in war is a result of human stupidity. But the great artist has this in common with the warrior, that he preaches a life more extended, more virile than commerce or manufacture can afford to her sons. To-day so much of our interest is concentrated upon the mere problems of living, of the difficulty of procuring enough food and clothing that it is almost an insult to ask us to waste our energy expending ecstatic joy over anything. Occasionally we revolt from our cramped and unnatural conditions, we burst out of the box, we have our Mafekings and our Peace nights, but for them we must have a reasonable excuse. All too soon ashamed at our " lack of self-control," we settle down to the humdrum of our existences as though we were cart-horses and not men ; and we call in the painters of soft sentiment to comfort us with futile visions of a life at which we know that we are too timid to clutch.

But Van Gogh shouts that, if we could awake, every life can be passionate and beautiful. He is like Redding, in *The Wild Duck* of Ibsen—he goes about torturing men with the claims of the " Ideal." More or less according to his ability, every artist is an exponent of a philosophy of wonder ; man before nature is no more than the child before a railway engine for the first time. But Van Gogh is not content to be a mere philosopher. He never was. In his early days he deserted a firm of art dealers to preach to the Belgian coal miners. He was too innately artist to continue to be a preacher, too innately evangelist not to remain prophet. He is a prophet of the disturbing magic of the world. As the street preacher hurts the sensibilities of the ladies who enjoy a comfortable religion under the direction of a well paid and soothing priest, so Van Gogh hurts the sensibilities of a public which has grown to look upon the artist as a panderer to moments of reposeful leisure. There is the same difference between a fashionable preacher and a Salvationist as between the fashionable portrait painter and Van Gogh.

Van Gogh is a sort of volcanic eruption occurring in a hitherto peaceably cultivated land. Because he felt that different colours have different emotional significance he does not hesitate to paint his friends' faces orange or green to indicate the quality of his attachment to them. His landscapes writhe with subterraneous life. This power of lending a fictitious sensation of real life to a dead canvas or statue is one which we will discuss later ; it arises out of design, and the life so produced has a strange effect of vital significance more powerful upon us than any exhibition of real life.

In a letter written to Emil Bernard, Van Gogh gives a description of a landscape seen from the Asylum for Nervous Diseases where he went voluntarily on account of hallucinations which followed sunstroke :

" . . . to the right a grey terrace, a piece of wall and a few faded rose trees, to the left the park ground (English red), the soil of which

Louvre

VAN GOGH
FLOWERS IN A BRASS VASE

is scorched by the sun and covered with pine needles. The edge of the park is planted with tall pine trees, the trunks and branches of which are English red and the green of which is all the more vivid for having a touch of black. These two stand out against the evening sky, the yellow ground of which is streaked with violet stripes. Higher up the yellow shades off into pink and then into green. A low wall, also English red, obstructs the view and is overtowered at one spot by a little violet and yellow ochre hill. The first tree has a gigantic trunk which has been struck and split by lightning ; one side branch alone still projects high up into the air and lets showers of dark green needles fall down. This gloomy giant—a vanquished hero—which one can regard as a living being is a strange contrast to the smile of a belated rose that is fading away on a rose-bush opposite. . . . The sky produces yellow reflections—after a shower —in a pool of water. In a ray of sunshine—the last reflection—the deep yellow ochre is intensified to a glowing orange. Dark figures steal in and out between the tree trunks. You can well imagine that this combination of red ochre, of green bedimmed with grey, and of black lines defining the forms, *may help to call forth the feeling of fright* which often seizes many of my fellow sufferers. . . . I have described (this) in order to show you that one can *give the impression of fear* without going direct to the historical Gethsemane. . . ."

In this description Van Gogh puts down clearly what he is trying to do. He is trying to create a super-nature. To people who go to pictures merely to have their previous impressions confirmed, or who desire to have defective imagination stimulated, the pictures of Van Gogh can have only an effect of shock. To appreciate his work we must realize that nature contains more than mere actuality, and that by means of art we can partake of visions more poignant than are our own. We must be willing to submit ourselves to the leadership of the artist, and penetrate through him into the land of reality.

Van Gogh's appreciation of nature is akin to that of the Chinese or Japanese. He is indeed somewhat more anthropomorphic, but he recognizes the affinity ; for in his letters he continually refers to the virtue of the " crêpe prints " and more than once says that he is trying to get a Japanese effect into his work. However, this Oriental element which creeps into Van Gogh is very different from the pseudo-Japanese work which has become popular in recent years. It depends not upon a mere imitation of technical device, for few people would accuse Van Gogh of imitating his " crêpe prints," but it lies in a recognition of the vision of similar values in nature.

The intensity of his sense of space, and the difference of attitude which exists between Van Gogh and the ordinary painter who is searching for the picturesque is illustrated in another extract from his correspondence :

" I have just done two large pen drawings, for instance, of a bird's-eye view of an endless plain seen from the top of a hill ; vineyards and fields of stubble reaching to infinity and extending like the surface of the sea to the horizon which is bounded by the hills of *La Cran*. It does not look Japanese but, truth to tell, I have never painted anything so essentially Japanese. A tiny figure of a labourer and a train running through the cornfields constitute the only signs of life in the picture. Think of it ! on one of my first days at this place a painter friend of mine said to me : ' It would be absurdly tedious to paint that ! ' I did not attempt to answer, but thought the spot so beautiful that I could not summon up the strength to upbraid the idiot. I returned to the locality again and again and made two drawings of it—this flat stretch of country which contains nothing save infinity, eternity."

The preacher in the street who calls to you to repent or go to hell cannot be delicate or mealy-mouthed, his message is too urgent ; nor could Van Gogh be delicate. His technique becomes a modification of that of the Pointillists, but the tedious spotting was impossible for his rabid temperament. One could not express the fierce joy of nature by a process of laying square spots. In consequence his colour stretches out into ribbons and whorls of interadjacent colours. If he cannot lay down his colour freshly enough with a brush, he squeezes it directly from the tube on to the canvas.

It is characteristic of the difference between the two men that Van Gogh could understand and admire Cézanne, but the old recluse of Arles thought Van Gogh a madman. " Vous êtes fou," said Cézanne bluntly to the Dutchman, who showed him some of his canvases. Cézanne represents the foundations, while Van Gogh is the banner waving from the uppermost pinnacle. Cézanne represents a method upon which a new classicism of art can be built. Van Gogh is an example of triumphant individuality. Cézanne's ideas even in the hands of a lesser man would have been fruitful to future generations ; Van Gogh's art in the hands of a lesser man would have been nonsense.

CHAPTER V

RENOIR

RENOIR is the third great figure which has its influence on the modern developments ; but, although he was a contemporary of Cézanne and preceded Van Gogh, I think it doubtful that the influence of Renoir became at all marked until a period later than either of the other two. Renoir has been merged into the Impressionist movement because he adopted the Impressionist ideas of a study of light, but he does not go any great way with the Impressionists. The Impressionists study light for light's sake—solidity, sense of mass, composition even, did not hold a place in their theory—but Renoir uses light and shadow deliberately for pattern-making as well as to emphasize the solidity of his figures. The Impressionist " light " is tinted air, but the light of Renoir is only a shimmer upon solid flesh.

There is little dispute to-day about Renoir's right to be called a master. His picture, " Les Parapluies," though by no means a perfect example of his best work, holds in the National Gallery a place level with the lesser works of the greatest masters.

Renoir is an example of the fact that there are no rules to govern a master. The artist, in general, revolts from the clamour of the public for pictures of pretty girls and of sentimental subjects. This revolt is the operation of an instinctive sense of self-protection. The borderland between a deadly prettiness and a real enduring beauty is so delicate that the average serious painter dares no more tread it than he dares walk along the coping of a high wall. If an artist has but a moderate power of producing works of æsthetic value, the more he fears to approach prettiness. If a man paints

48

stern and undesirable subjects, then any hint of beauty which he can
put into his art shines the more brightly in contrast with his surroundings, like a jewel upon a heap of pebbles.   But, if the same
man attempt a pretty subject, then his art will be in danger of being
swamped by the tawdry attractions of his model, his art then suffers
as a jewel would suffer upon a heap of glass gauds. But if your
jewel is a Koh-i-noor you need not fear whether it lie upon pebbles
or upon gauds.

One cannot hold that an artist always is at this best.   He follows
a wavering course which is dictated by his digestion, his love affairs,
his financial worries and other irritants or stimulants.   Quite a
third of the works of any master are interesting only as relics,
treasurable as rarities.   But even the bad work of a good man is
noteworthy for a certain dignity or austerity, or some other quality
which marks it from the mass of its fellows.   Renoir's worst work is
almost fit for the tops of chocolate boxes.

One can eat a badly cooked beefsteak with more relish than an ill-
made sweet.   When Renoir's Koh-i-noor is clouded, the gewgaws
overwhelm it with their cheap glitter.

But when his genius glows most brightly it is of a fine water
which outshines the glass in which he has chosen to set it.

Renoir is a painter of women, a painter of luscious rather than
pretty women.   He has said : " If women had no breasts I would
not have painted them."   He goes back to the old Greek religion
of the worship of the flesh, and there is indeed not a little of the
Greek spirit in his art.   One can imagine him walking along with an
Athenian procession, one can imagine him even as standard bearer
to Dionysus.   But he is not valuable as an artist because he paints
pretty women, and florescent maidenhood, but because he endows
these images of his with a supreme vitality, and because of the
subtlety of his colour.   Renoir in his best work is the Titian of the
Impressionist movement.   Indeed, there are many points of
relationship between the Old Master's " Bacchus and Ariadne "
in the National Gallery and the " Bathers " of Renoir.

E

We may now—in connection with Renoir's contribution to the modern movements—make a short survey of some questions of movement and the presentation of life in art. It is well known that the eye is a sort of camera, a camera on a ball and socket joint controlled by muscles, so that it may, within limits, be at once directed at any object of interest. Instinctively any object which invites interest is focused so that the image is brought to the centre of the retina where it may be most clearly perceived. When we gaze fixedly at any one point the objects surrounding are still perceptible by us, though not clearly seen. When we look at any object of size, the different parts of the object are successively brought to the centre of the retina for consideration and the eye is in continuous though almost imperceptible motion. This is the case not only in looking at real objects but when picturing mental images. The movement of the eye is instinctive and unconscious—persons who have suffered from inflammation of the iris have told me that they have been forced to hold their minds blank of images owing to the torture caused by this unconscious movement of the eye in following mental images. Three sets of muscles control this movement. The eye moves freely from side to side, but with more difficulty up and down, and when the vertical movement is at all large the head must be moved; thus, vertical movement of the eye demands a much more conscious co-ordination of the muscle than the horizontal movement.

If we consider these movements in relation to certain well known shapes, we shall perceive an apparent relationship between emotional effect and the physical reactions of the shape in question. First let us compare a circle and an oval or ellipse. The circle is a satisfying figure, excellently complete, but the interest in it is soon exhausted. The eye travels about the circumference and comes to rest at the centre. Here there is a feeling of equality of pull from every part of the circumference, which causes satisfaction, but the eye has no further inducement to muscular movement. With the ellipse the eye travels over the circumference with more interest than over the circumference of the circle. The quality of the curve is continually changing. We get a sense of great variety combined with a pleasing inverted repetition. The eye also finally may come to rest at the centre of gravity, but the value of the ellipse is not yet exhausted. The varied pull of the proportions is still felt. The eye is tempted to move and to re-analyse the curves and balances. The figure holds a considerable preponderance of interest over the circle, and it will be noted that the preponderance of interest about equals the muscular temptation to movement. The interest in the ellipse, however, varies with the direction of its long diameter. The horizontal has an emotional quality different from that of the vertical ellipse. The eye moves easily from side to side, and thus the horizontal ellipse is more easily grasped than the vertical. In the horizontal figure the comparison between length and breadth is made with ease. The long vertical proportion of the upright oval is grasped with more muscular co-operation, and this difference of muscular expenditure, though unconsciously applied, seems to be reflected in the sentiment regarding the two figures. There is a more natural approval of the horizontal, it gives a feeling of restfulness and of great stability. A second factor increases the differences of interest between the two figures. We are all under the unconscious domination of gravity. The horizontal line does not awaken in a lively fashion our sense of stability, for it represents the final stable position, but the upright diagram presents to us another stability which is set in the midst of instability. All upright lines and figures have a charm of delicate *balance* which is lacking from horizontal ones.

There is, then, in the horizontal figure an ease of grasp, and a satisfactory sense of stability ; in the vertical we find more difficulty of grasp but a corresponding increase of interest because of balance which seems to be an inherent quality. From the former figure we get a sensation of peace, from the latter a feeling of dignity and of inherent power. It will be further found that this more or less applies to all horizontal and vertical figures, and that each has a significance which is seemingly allied to the muscular action and sense of balance which is called into play by them.

It must further be recognized that the difference which exists between the circle, the oval, etc., has nothing to do with that quality of desirability which we have examined with reference to corrugated iron. We do not desire the one figure more than the other. Nor have they their essential value from the associations. We do not connect the circle with a round face, nor the ellipse with an oval one, and thus at second-hand derive emotional values. The figure carries in itself the significance because of what it is, and is not allied to any perceptible predilection. The qualities of such a nature may be called " abstract."

The linear shape has, however, another property, that of suggesting movement. Let us consider another diagram ; a straight line which meets another straight line at an angle :

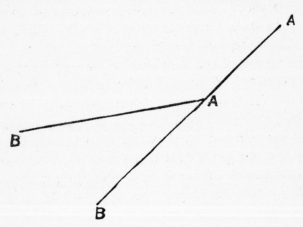

If we consider this figure dispassionately it will be found that there is a tendency for the eye to travel from A towards B, and that it does not take the reverse path from B to A with similar ease. If we now separate the diagram into two angles we find that when the acute angle has been removed the eye travels either arm of the obtuse figure easily enough, from A to B or from B to A without preference. But with the acute angle the effect remains. The eye travels easily from A to B, it has to be forced from B to A, and the effort becomes increasingly pronounced as the angle grows narrower. We find in the acute angle a strong inducement for the eye to travel in one direction only. This produces a curious physiological effect. We are all aware of the sensation which is felt as a steamer leaves the quay, or when sitting in a train another train begins to move. There is a tendency to transfer some of the motion perceived to the other partner of the two *relatively moving* systems. Thus, the quay seems suddenly to be imbued with movement, or we feel that our own train has started. The same phenomenon is felt at the acute angle. The eye is seduced into definite movement, and the diagram

borrows an illusive power of movement in the opposing direction. The same is true, but in a lesser degree, of the obtuse angle. Although the eye can travel from A to B or from B to A, the sense of motion suggested at the apex of the angle is quite perceptible, and the figure has a tendency to urge forward. In a lesser degree the curve possesses a similar property. The curve, like the angle, has the property of movement, only the curve creates a modified sensation.

If we depict a series of obtuse angles as in the diagram, it will be noted that each angle has a tendency to urge outwards at its own apex. Then results a general sensation of urging forwards, but also a general tendency to spread *outwards* in all directions. In the curve this tendency is distributed equally to all parts, there is a suggestion of movement and a suggestion of power to increase.   As in the angle, the more rapid the curvature the more eager the sense of movement. This suggests another point of emotional difference between the circle and the oval.   The circle is evenly balanced, the tendency to movement is equalized all round ; but with the ellipse the finer curves at the ends have more dynamic power than the broader curve of the sides.   The oval thus seems to possess powers of stretching itself in the direction of the greatest length.

These properties of movement-suggestion are used by every artist.   The most obvious form, the device of the comic draughts-man, of placing divergent lines behind a figure which is supposed to be in motion is well known to everybody.   But how far-reaching and important is this principle is not generally understood.   The quality of suggested movement is one of the most valuable in Art. The power of organizing forms which seem to possess an internal power of movement mark out the great artist from the smaller.   By it he determines how his picture shall be seen by the spectator.

The essential difference which marks the art of painting from that of music is that the former is seen in space, the latter in time.   The musician can calculate his harmonies in a definite order ; but it appears at first as if the painter cannot do this.   It would seem that he must invent schemes which are harmonious and equally valuable seen in any order, considered one after another in the most haphazard of ways.   But owing to his power of suggesting movement to the eye the great artist can to some extent control the order in which his harmonies are appreciated.   It is true that at the first glance the picture is understood in all its general aspects.   But once the eye begins a more detailed examination it considers successively the different parts, and the picture becomes a work in " time."   Like a poem it is then appreciated section after section.   The inefficient artist who cannot create an organized sensation of movement has no means of controlling the travel of the eye about his work.   If he wishes to make any part of his work important, he must emphasize the light falling upon it or use a brutal colour to attract attention.

But the great artist by his use of the instinctive eye movement in response to certain forms does, within limits, lead the interest of the spectator through his picture in a deliberate path, and it is by the successive grasp of certain parts one after another that the spectator completes his acquaintance with the picture. There results from this a sense of an order more complete than is found in life, for life has no such organic movement inducing forms—they *may* occur in life, but are chance and haphazard.

This sense of greater order lends a heightened value to whatever is depicted. For a while we share the mentality of the artist. The harmonious succession of shapes, of colours, of light and shade, of movement to and fro, in and out, puts us in contact with something which is more consistent, more complete, and therefore more valuable and satisfying than the often chaotic nature which we normally perceive.

Not only does the artist use this quality of movement to seduce the eye into appreciating his work in the manner and in the order in which he wishes, but he can very materially influence the mood of the spectator by his suggestions. The acute angle produces quick movement, the obtuse slow, the curve gives sensations of exuberance, the upright line dignity and power, the horizontal restfulness. By a judicial use of these devices, the eye is to some extent under the physical control of the artist not only in direction but in speed. By a suitable combination of form he can induce the emotional value which he desires for his work, but he can hasten over one part, slow down in another. Like the musician he plays his tempo and the senses follow his baton. The use of such devices, however, must be subtle and not immediately obvious. Nothing is more disturbing in a poem than a too pedantic insistence upon the mechanical precision of the line, or in music a too rigid adherence to the construction of the bar. So in painting when the work is too palpably *constructed;* the eye quickly loses its interest and finds the work tedious and manufactured.

As certain shapes are more interesting than others, so we may say that certain shapes have more beauty than have others. We have said that the oval is more interesting than the circle. Interest does not necessarily predicate Beauty. But I think that the difference of physical interest between the circle and the ellipse is a difference of interest in beauty. It is a perception of qualities which when perceived gives pleasure. The varying proportions of the oval arouse interest and pleasure; some ovals are capable of arousing more satisfaction than others. Some curves which are not purely geometrical are capable of giving a more intense pleasure than the geometrical curve of an oval. There have been attempts made to work out the most beautiful type of curve. Hogarth wrote a treatise called " The Analysis of Beauty," and sets perfect beauty in an S-formed curve in which one gets an inverted rhythmical repetition. The curve, he states, should be between the swelling which are extravagant and the flat which are stiff. The question of beauty, however, is too complex to be reduced thus to a single formula, it must vary slightly with every one, since it is to some extent at least physiological and part psychical, neither of which parts is constant in humanity.

The fact remains, however, that as the senses thrill at certain combinations of colour so they react to the appreciation of rhythmical relationships in line. The shape of the Greek and of the Chinese vase is beautiful whether we consider it as a vase or as a curve. The beauty of a line or of a curve seems in some way allied with muscular balances, repetitions of movement, and so on. As long as one line remains isolated these balances operate among themselves, and we can say that the line has intrinsic beauty. If, however, another line is brought near, or any other object which attracts attention, a new set of balances is evoked. We now receive an interchange between the two; the values are altered, as though a weight were to be cast into the pan of an evenly swinging scale. Each line affects the other. Each line is modified in emotional value by its interactions with the other. Two parallel lines can be rendered apparently not parallel by the interference of diagonals, and though this is the extreme case it illustrates interlinear inter-ference in a way which is undeniable. By this means a line beautiful in itself can be rendered almost ugly by the introduction of some line which destroys, while the beauty may be enhanced by a line which emphasizes the balances. Thus, we find that the curves of the two sides of a Chinese vase make a more beautiful system when, as they are in nature, opposite and complementing each other, than if only one side is considered alone : while an opposition of two of Hogarth's " lines of Beauty " could be arranged to destroy the quality which is inherent in each.

Of course the four chief controlling lines of a composition are constituted by the frame. Whatever linear harmonies we place together upon the canvas we cannot forget that these must also harmonize with the limiting edges of the picture. This institutes a great difference between nature and art, for nature has no frame. This consideration of the harmonic use of the limits of the frame is specially remarkable in Renoir. His *mise-en-page* is almost always superlative. In no other artist can it be studied with more ease and with more satisfaction.*

But not only does the artist suggest a path for the eye through his picture, not only does he interweave forms which produce a sensation of pleasure—which is beauty—but by means of his control of movement-inducing forms he suggests life in his images. Cézanne, on the whole, is a master of the rigid line, his forms are as archi-tectural and as solid as a Romanesque building, he introduces his curve with care in order to emphasize the stability of his con-ception; Van Gogh uses lines which are in nervous movement and which give a strange restlessness to all that he touches. You have seen how growing flowers writhe in the cinematograph ; Van Gogh's line has the same quality. He has penetrated to this serpentine movement by intuition. Probably if we could invent a

* In art schools great harm is done to the sensibility of the students because the masters do not insist first of all upon a careful placing of the drawing upon the sheet of drawing paper.

cinematograph camera which would take photographs over a sufficiently extended period we would find that even the earth writhes
in a similar way. Van Gogh gives voice to this strange, almost
torturing sense of growth. Renoir, on the other hand, flows in the
large and satisfying curve. His shapes express just that quality of
emotion which made him paint the nude woman. There is a strange
palpitating sense of movement in his figures, which is created by the
flowing and interlocking rhythm of his constructions. This magnificence of sweep, combined with a colour sense rich in the contrasts
of warm Southern flesh tints and blue, gives to Renoir a Titianesque
richness at once sensuous and satisfying.

These rich curved forms Renoir fills in with solid forms which
are the contrary of Cézanne's. Cézanne reduces nature more or
less to inter-acting flattened surfaces, Renoir emphasizes the
spherical and the cylinder. Cézanne uses the spherical to accent
and contrast with his planes, Renoir uses the plane to accent his
cylinders. Cézanne aims at austerity, Renoir at sensuousness.

CHAPTER VI

GAUGUIN

freedom vitality

GAUGUIN, half Frenchman, half Creole, is the fourth figure at the head of the new non-representative impulse in art. As a boy he ran away to sea, returned, settled down into bourgeois life, became a successful banker, and then, suddenly, plunged into art, deserting his wife and family; founded what is known as the Pont Aven school, a direct reaction against the creed of the Impressionists, and finally, in the hope of discovering a true primitive simplicity, went to Tahiti, where he turned native, and died, the only witness of his death being an old ex-cannibal. Both Cézanne and Van Gogh are figures of romance: Cézanne because of his single-minded devotion to art, which turned him into such a recluse that many of the younger men almost imagined him to be a fabulous or mythical figure; Van Gogh because of his dynamic personality, because of the flame of passion for Nature which consumed him up, and which was responsible for his final madness and suicide. But neither Cézanne nor Van Gogh was deliberately romantic, they were unconscious of this element in themselves; it is quite absent from their work. Gauguin, however, is a self-conscious romantic. After his first visit to Polynesia he returned clad in an extravagant costume, expecting to take Paris by storm. But because his romanticism was genuine, because he was not content as are too many merely to dream or to paint ideals, but endeavoured with all his courage to live them, because this romanticism was not merely a sensuous refuge from an inadequate life, but a striving towards the realization of an ideal of more free existence, Gauguin's art has the value which comes from all positive expression of real vitality.

Though their ideals and ideas of life and resultant techniques were very different, the attitude of these three men towards art was of a similar nature, and springs from the same impulses. Each one strives to create the sensation of a world of which *he* is conscious, he does not try to re-represent the world which everybody more or less takes for granted. In Cézanne what we would call the anthropomorphic value is almost absent; his wife, two or three pears, a landscape, or some nude women bathing, each subject, no matter what it is, has an apparently equal significance, he infuses everything with the magic of reality; the sense of wonder lies poignant in everything. His problem is to seek out, to penetrate the meaning, to present it as æsthetic form, as space, as Arabesque, as colour. In Van Gogh not so much reality as his own ecstasy for reality moves the artistic impulse. " *Merely* landscapes " are not enough; what the landscape means to him, what are his reactions, is the important factor. Because to him the fields surged with hidden life and hinted meanings, he finds a form and a colour technique which will make these things patent to others. He paints the head of a dear friend orange against a blue background, because orange is a warm passionate colour, and because the remoteness and chill of the blue will further intensify the suggestion. In Cézanne there is no hint of what we call literature. What Cézanne has to say can be said, imagined and experienced in no medium other than that of painting. But Van Gogh is not altogether dissociated from this literary content. In the extract from his letter from the hospital he himself puts into literary form the *idea* of a picture—his letters are often quite exquisite literature. But no literary content can re-create the violence and power of Van Gogh's visions. One may say that a field surges with hidden life, yet arouse no response in the imaginations of the readers, but when beneath one's eye the life appears to be almost bursting out we reach a point of visual art with which no literature can vie. This quality also appears in Van Gogh's drawings.

But in Gauguin, though his line has simplicity and dignity, it is by his colour that he really creates a true " æsthetic paraphrase " of what is fundamentally a poetic idea.   And in this, curiously enough, though the most like to the Chinese in technique, and in his woodcuts he is very Oriental, Gauguin is not actually so close as Van Gogh to the spirit which move the best Oriental artists to expression.

The art of Gauguin has been called Atavistic.   It is imagined that his return to savagery was the result of his Creole blood, and that inherently he was half savage.   Rather, I think he was too civilized.   He was so civilized that he could regard this civilization as a fraud.   Whereas to the savage it is heaped marvel.   He writes to Strindberg :

" Your civilization is your disease, my barbarism my restoration to health.   The ' Eve ' of your civilized conception makes us nearly all mysogynists.   The old Eve who shocked you in my studio will perhaps seem less odious to you some day.   I have perhaps been unable to do more than suggest my world, which seems unreal to you. . . . Only the Eve I have painted can stand naked before us. Yours would always be shameless in this natural state, and if beautiful the source of pain and of evil. . . ."

Gauguin is, in reality, a relative of More, of Swift, of William Morris and of every dreamer who, dissatisfied with this reality of life as it is lived, has tried to picture a new, more healthy existence. Gauguin alone had the temerity to seek for a concrete example of his ideal.   In the Marquesas he found, not what he was seeking, but something remotely pointing towards the object of his search. In his painting he strives to give to his ideal a form more concrete still.

The major part of his canvases express either dignity, repose, or a sense of the mysterious, the linear scheme simple but often very unusual in conception.   His figures express an extraordinary stability borrowed from the Egyptians, his landscapes are stripped of all accidentals, often re-invented and reduced to the most simple of formulæ. At one time he called himself a " synthesist." This is only a generalization of his whole life. He desired to rid everything of accidentals and to get down to the stark innocence of nature. He thus rejects the analytical method of the Impressionists. He ignores the accidentals of light as did Cézanne, but for a very different reason. He says, " If I wish to express greenness, a metre of green is more green than a centimetre."

His line, too, opens an interesting question in the art of drawing. Gauguin's custom, at last, was not to alter a line once he had put it down. He said that before the line was drawn an artist had a mental conception of what he wished to put down, but that once the line was upon paper, that which had been drawn, however imperfect it might be, had destroyed the conception which lay in the mind of the artist : that any alteration of this first drawn line could not really represent genuine correction, but only the fumbling after an ideal which had been lost ; that thenceforth the artist was, as it were, but stumbling about in the dark, hoping by luck to recapture something which had escaped from him. If we persist in considering drawing merely as copying a fact, this idea is of course absurd. But a large truth lies behind, if we think of it as representing an image which exists in the mind alone, and only based upon nature. In this case the drawn expression does destroy, or does materially alter the mental image, and an attempt to correct usually spoils, without recapturing any more than that which we had at first seized.

Gauguin brings less discovery to the new movement than Van Gogh or Cézanne or Renoir. He was as much poet as painter, and his mind harks back to an ideal past which he would force into the present. Thus he as much reasserts the value of the arts of past civilizations (as those of Egypt or Japan) as enlarges the power of the artists of the future. But this insistence on the value of æsthetic process which had been neglected is not without its value. Art seems to be in a state of continual forgetfulness. We do not seem able to hold on to those things which our predecessors have used with so much virtue. The Egyptians showed the value of imagina-

GAUGUIN
WOMAN'S HEAD

tive form right at the beginning of the history of art (as we know it), but how often since has the dignity of the Egyptian imagination been equalled ? The Persians showed the value of colour. It seems almost impossible that from Titian and Rubens we should sink to Bouguereau or David. Not only must we strive forward to the future, but we have continually to reassert the value of the past. If we lose hold of either we lose our sense of proportion.

Cézanne links up with the past on account of his fine sense of design, he steps away from it with his new sense of drawing and his insistence upon space composition. Gauguin teaches technically the arts both of Egypt and of Japan. He, too, would see man as something Godlike, something more stable than mere peripatetic man. Like both the older arts, his was a rhythmic decoration, the space in his works being often suggestion rather than statement, he boldly invents conventions which are as accurate as a line of prose description and which omit as much. Yet though Cézanne has now become the idol, the Giotto of the modern movements, Gauguin has often had the prior influence. The three most powerful exponents of the modern movement, Matisse, Picasso and Derain, all came into modern art through the impulse, not of Cézanne, but of Gauguin. The reason for this is that Cézanne is too subtle and his problems are too difficult for the young painter who has been trained in the æsthetic outlook of the past century. The mind must be prepared to understand him. Gauguin entices not because of his strength, but because of the barbaric colour, the lure of the primeval. In this world of ultra-civilization in which we fear to live valiantly, these pictures of an apparently idyllic existence have seduction and charm. Gauguin first attracts by his literature; but his literature would not have been effectual were it not embodied in a form which makes his intention vital. If Bouguereau had gone to Tahiti he would have caused no stir, for the technique of Bouguereau has nothing to do with savagery.

Gauguin entices by the suitability of his methods to his context. This is the true art of illustration. Gauguin is an almost ideal

illustrator. But those disciples who came into the modern movements through Gauguin soon learned his limitations. They pass on
by degrees to Cézanne and from him learn that they have to leap
forwards for themselves. But a host of others came in also clinging
to Gauguin's skirts. Many of these were lazy persons who wished
to paint without the struggle of learning academic drawing, others
were ambitious and wanted to *faire du neuf*. So that Gauguin,
though himself a considerable artist, has probably been responsible
for more bad artists and more spoiled canvas than any one other
painter in the history of the world save Raphael.

But Gauguin brings to the surface a problem which remained for
the younger school to develop to its full. This was the problem of
pure colour. Colour had been coming up to a real importance for
a long while. Delacroix is a colour advance on Courbet, Manet
goes beyond Delacroix. The Impressionists, especially Monet,
begin to perceive colour as something positive to be enjoyed for
its own sake. Van Gogh frankly deserts realistic colour in order
to use its emotional qualities.

Gauguin with his " metre of green " raises a new problem in the
art of European painting. Nobody had ever wanted to express
" greenness " before. Gauguin recognized that a picture can have
the same colour ideal as a Persian carpet. Indeed with the rough
canvases that he used he often arrived at a textile surface which
makes one think of tapestry rather than of painting.

CHAPTER VII

ART AND THE NEW CIVILIZATION

WE may rest for a moment to consider both the causes and effects of this new spirit which was growing up in art. Cézanne, Van Gogh, Seurat, Renoir, Gauguin and Signac constitute the advance movement of the modern developments; they are the *grandfathers* of the Independents of to-day. Rousseau, the customs-house officer, comes in as a detached figure standing somewhat apart. Of these revolutionaries not one is living now. The *fathers*, most of whom are alive to-day, include such men as Matisse, Derain, Vlaminck, Picasso, Bracque, Utrillo, Bonnard, Modigliani, Friesz, Marie Laurencin, Gontcharova and many others, of most of whom we hope to treat as we reach the different points of view which we wish to clear up. The *sons* are every day becoming more numerous, more conscious, more powerful. The art of Europe, which has remained almost stable since the fourteenth century, has been revolutionized within some fifty years. This new conception of art is becoming rapidly a popular conception. The illustrative art in the daily and weekly press of Europe is losing the conventionalisms of the academy. The imitative representation is being more and more reserved for the camera. The illustrator is being freed, and the public appreciation is being educated by the popular press. Even England, despite the Academy, has contributed to the movement.

Art is often regarded as a sort of detached occupation pursued by gifted—and sometimes wilful, wicked and wrong-headed—men, whose productions should be meant either for advertising, for amusement, or else for the delight of those rich enough to purchase works of art. Kings were the artists' greatest patrons, but unfortunately for the artist it seems to be no longer respectable for kings to possess great treasures closed up for their private enjoyment. Kings have been democratized, and the pictures collected for kingly delight have gone the road of their owners. Thus we become possessed of the nucleus of our public collections. However, since the kings and the art have followed the same path, the connection between the arts and the luxurious has been fairly strongly held. Art is still generally considered to be the luxurious refuge of the tired or bored rich. Few will admit more than this.

Art is in reality a sort of social thermometer telling the spiritual condition of humanity, as the clinical tube beneath the tongue betrays the physical state. Some persons, who have seen something of this, have exaggerated the functions and power of art. They state that Van Gogh, Matisse, Nietzsche, Ibsen, Stravinsky and others were the prime promoters of the war. That the revolution in art swinging a wider circle turned to national unrest and eventually to national catastrophe. This would be equivalent to saying that the rising of the thermometer had made the day hotter.

All these varied manifestations of art are independently springing from the same source. In a note to his *Quintessence of Ibsenism*, Bernard Shaw quotes the remark of a German woman who accused him of plagiarizing from Nietzsche before he had ever heard of that philosopher. Shaw adduces it as evidence of a world-wide artistic impulse which gave birth to Schopenhauer, Wagner, Ibsen, Nietzsche and Strindberg, and " which would have found expression if every one of these writers had perished in his cradle."

This artistic upheaval is but a reflection of social conditions, and is in logical harmony with a general mental surge forward which has taken place during the last century. One may almost say that the old order died on the Field of Waterloo. If our great-grandfathers could be brought back in the flesh they would find a civilization totally distinct from that in which they died. The change from the stage-coach to the flying-machine, from the sailing-ship to the

Oceanic, from the guns of the *Victory* to Big Bertha, from the hand loom to the cotton factory would constitute a revolution compared with which the artistic revolution would appear modest in the extreme. Even in that rigid body, the Church, the parson from a poor clerk who might with luck marry the squire's housekeeper has developed into a village autocrat of whom the squire may stand in awe.

Napoleon is the last great figure of the civilization which came into being during the Renaissance, but which had its beginning in Rome and in Greece, where also its arts were rooted. Fulton, who offered Napoleon a steamship with which to invade England, is the forerunner of the new era in material matters, while Schopenhauer with his " World as mind and projection " opens the door of the new mental and artistic developments. David and Ingres are the Napoleonic painters who mark the close of that culture, the beginnings of which is best represented by Leonardo da Vinci—although one might by leaping the Gothic period stretch it back to the Greek artist Apelles who has been considered by some as the first artist to initiate the degeneration of painting by the introduction of perspective and of deceptive imitation ; but who has been praised, on the other hand, for a realism which fable narrates reached to so high a pitch that the very birds tried to peck his painted fruit. From Lorenzo the Magnificent until the Battle of Waterloo stretches a practically homogeneous civilization in which nothing alters save slight improvements of which the means were already at hand. The world moved from one period to the other either by leg or by horse-power, commerce was low ; most of the necessities and even the luxuries of life were produced in the home ; every country could nourish the whole of its inhabitants. For a period of five centuries, though there was nothing to inhibit invention, hardly one practical idea for the simplification of life, save the clock, was evolved. The art which matched and decorated this period shows a similar stability. An art is living only as long as it grows in harmony with its social conditions.

The succeeding period is marked by a struggle of the new conditions with the old. The new conditions trying to liberate themselves are bound down by conventions adapted to those which were rapidly passing away. As H. G. Wells says in *Anticipations :* " before every railway train prances the ghost of an old horse." This period is matched in art by that which separates Ingres from the Impressionists. It is an attempt to fill old wine skins with new wine. Some of the skins hold well enough, such as Delacroix and Manet, but others are sadly leaky ; we can no longer swallow the sentimentalism of Corot or the bombast of Turner, though we now appreciate their less ambitious works.

The idea which underlies the Post-Leonardo Academism is outlined in his treatise on the Art of Painting. It is " curiosity regarding the facts of nature's appearance, and the means of presenting them." Every painter is supposed to be explaining nature ideally. It is in its essentials a descriptive art, an analytic art. It is curiosity. Ruskin praises Turner because he explains more facts more clearly than has any other painter. Five thousand facts have been depicted about nature, and he's a genius who can present the five hundredth and first. Thus, apart from certain exceptions, this art is not inventive, as its society was also not inventive. It is a period which is slowly preparing for something ; living on its own fat like a bear in the winter-time.

The seventy years which bring us to the present day enclose an extraordinary social and practical upheaval. Before then, everything came from the cornucopia of Mother Nature and her seasons, man was to all intents and purposes a parasite upon the vegetable world. To-day, save for the essentials of nourishment and of clothing, man is freeing himself from the accidentals of external nature. Man no longer is moulded by and subjected to the chances of the seasons. He is gaining a mastery. He is learning to dispense more and more with the vegetable and even with the animal. One does not wish to suggest that the whole of this new driving force comes from the use of coal and the discovery of steam power.

These inventions are but part of the surge forward. A steam engine had been invented in Greek Alexandria, and coal was known as fuel long before it became important.   But we cannot fail to see a thread which runs through the whole movement of the world. The mechanics and inventions which re-create a world fashioned out of man's brain ; the philosophies which show the world as an image in the mind ; the novels and poems which now are becoming dramas of thought and of spiritual contest rather than of action ; the pictures of Van Gogh and of Cézanne ; the medical discoveries of the influence of the mind upon physical conditions ; and, lastly, the scientific demonstration that solid matter itself is composed of something which is not matter at all, something imponderable, immaterial : all these are intimately related in idea.

We see here that within a meagre century the whole of civilization has been altered because we no longer take nature for granted ; because we have declined to take nature for granted ; because we super-impose ourselves on nature.   Even if we are inclined to cry out for the good old days, we cannot deny the substitution which has occurred.   Man who was the slave of nature, the parasite of the horse, has to some extent freed himself, and daily his bonds are loosening.   He has practically imposed himself on nature.   Necessarily, because his art must be an echo of his time, in his art he also must impose himself upon nature.   It is quite useless to moan that nature is good enough for us.   It is untrue.   Every day we are kicking one of nature's offsprings with its limitations out of the door, and all the while we are struggling to find boots with which to kick out the others.   Man is fighting to free himself from the limitations of nature.   Art, which is often prophecy, has already unconsciously shown this fact.

These various movements in practical, in scientific, and in artistic ideas are not inter-creative. Van Gogh is not trying to illustrate Schopenhauer.   Each movement is spontaneous and grows up in its particular craft, ignorant of its intimate connection with what is growing up elsewhere.   This proves that it belongs to a general mental move and to a new and instinctively forming conception of nature which differs widely from that of the Renaissance.

The great problem with which man now is presented is that of piercing beneath the problem of life. We are still bound by the saying, "Nothing living save from life." But everywhere the researches are directed towards finding the first causes. The artist himself is penetrating the secrets of his art. He can no longer be content to work by instinct. Cézanne, Renoir, Van Gogh, Gauguin and Seurat each develop a part of the consciousness of the structure of pictorial presentation which has illuminated the vision of the whole European art.

In Spain the people have a habit of seasoning their dishes with red peppers (*pimiento*) of a strong and a peculiar flavour. The Spaniard would not appreciate a plain chicken boiled without this relish. It would have no flavour for him. There are many travellers, however, who can appreciate the unadulterated flavour of chicken, to get the subtle delight of which they would forgo the pleasures of *pimiento*. The value of the dish may lie in the cookery; but the prime value of the dish lies in the meat. Fine cookery tends more and more to bring out the value and flavour of the meat itself, rather than to impose upon it extraneous flavourings.

The painter has now been trying to pierce down to the meat of art, to those things which depend upon painting alone. One does not attempt to deny that extraneous flavourings and sauces have their own charm, and that painting does not always depend solely upon the quality of its meat. But there is a danger that flavourings may go out of fashion and taste. To-day we cannot understand the strange condiments of the food of the Middle Ages, we cannot now eat dishes flavoured with ambergris. But chicken remains chicken. The artist who is seeking for the root matters of art, the things which belong to painting and to nothing else, is trying to find something which will be beyond the chances of taste or of fashion. Owing to the cast of his civilization and to the mental bias of the present day the artist is seeking these permanencies rather within himself than from without.   But he always remains an ego facing something which is external, and his ego can only communicate with other egos by means of this joint external element " nature," therefore the artist will draw his primary inspiration from this common source.   If he draws too far within himself, if he becomes *too* personal, he risks the danger of becoming as unintelligible as a man who invents a language which nobody else can decipher.   This danger faces some modern artists.

It is a curious fact that, while England has been the prime mover and, with America, the prime inventor of this new civilization, these countries are the centres of the chief resistance which is offered to the art which springs from the civilizations which they have created.   Modern art, as it is called, is no longer a question of discussion in Europe, it is an accepted fact.   The Post-Leonardo Academism is likely to die with the present generation.   The immobility of England, as a whole, is worth a moment's analysis. We are a strange people.   We have a certain distrust and disdain for the works of intelligence, and yet have produced some of the finest intelligences in the history of Europe.   In consequence we tend to use these intelligences for tasks beneath their merit.   We have a lust for opening tins and, instead of taking a tin-opener to them, we will use a scalpel.   We make Sir Isaac Newton chief of the Royal Mint ; there is our intellectual history in a line.

In consequence of this disdain for intelligence, we do not press forward to keep in touch with the most advanced thinking of the world.   We allow it to filter gradually down to us through various stages of dilution and journalism and, in consequence, popular ideas are almost always some fifty or sixty years behind the times.   Darwin and Spenser were popular authors in Russia while known only in the notorious distortions of the press in England ; Shakespeare is better known in Germany—where his works are played without cuts—than in his native land ; Wilde has had a greater influence upon French literature than on English.

In addition to this mental inertia we are not essentially a painting nation.   We are poetic first, musical afterwards, and painters last of all.   Our painters are accidents.   If we except the Spanish primitive " George, the Englishman," of whose actual nationality we cannot be certain, there is very little English painting which counts before Hogarth.   We are the only European nation which does or has not painted its houses.   Indeed, our understanding of painting is first of all literary.   The literature of art in the English language is formidable in amount and, upon the whole, foolish in quality. Almost invariably it has considered painting as a handmaiden of literature.   English painting has always been story-telling in paint ; the sort of thing that the Italians cast off with Giotto.   Even the important school of English water-colour painters from Maltby to Turner is a topographical school, a substitute for the book of travels. This point of view on art in England is admirably illustrated in a work on " Composition " which is the most popular amongst English art students.   This book opens, " We use figures because they are characters in a story. . . ."   Out of twenty-one chapters in that book, only two, and those the sketchiest, have anything to do with pure pictorial art, the remaining nineteen being concerned with story-telling or antique lore.   There is in addition an appendix which consecrates twenty-one pages to " Emblems and Texts," seventeen pages to " Mottoes " (clichés such as " A good beginning makes a good ending," or " Like master like man," or " Ars longa, vita brevis "), and seven pages to " Armour."   If such is the principal handbook for the use of students, it is not strange that art in England trails at least half a century behind the times.   The whole mental outlook of this book is that the task of the artist is that of painting *pastiches* of past centuries, and, like the child who writes " this is a man," that the artist, a naturally ignorant man, must be helped in his inadequacy with texts, mottoes, or poetical titles.

The foreigner would perceive in that book a cynical admission that the English student can never hope to be a painter, that there is no artistic meat in England, and that in consequence we must be fed upon sauces.

We see art through the literature of fifty years ago. But, although this is a book about art, I say that art cannot be understood through literature. It must be understood by the eyes and by the instincts alone, and until it is so understood there is no true appreciation of painting. Literature is only useful for loosening inhibitions which we place upon the optical sensibility.

In addition to this literary outlook upon the art of painting, we suffer more than any other country from a certain deformation of character, an elephantiasis of development which has made us concentrate almost exclusively upon sport as the one worthy occupation of leisure. " *Mens sana in corpore sano* " say our schoolmasters. As, however, I hope to show later, sport is in some sort a substitute for art, reaching its highest effects through similar channels and directed towards the same end, although the effects are of a much lower order. Unfortunately public appreciation has been seized by the " sane body," and imagines that the healthily developed mind is a necessary result. The Latin, however, placed the mind first in his aphorism ; we would place it last. The result is that mental development, and, above all, artistic development, is disdained in comparison with muscular virtues. This disdain coupled with the connection which is supposed to exist between art and luxury has made up the English idea of the artist, which is that he is a sort of weakling and serious jester at the court of riches.

CHAPTER VIII

THE DESIGNING INSTINCT

[handwritten margin note: original design lost but each ind. adds his own.]

ART separates into two definite and almost antagonistic divisions: the imitative and the imaginative. The imitative can be achieved, within the limits of painting, without touching the imaginative; while the latter may reach its brightest points without becoming imitative in any respect. But though one may say that these two divisions are antagonistic they are not in practice quite independent of each other. The imitative instinct is well known; the native throws stones at the monkey in order to make the animal fling coco-nuts in return, and more or less this imitating tendency stretches out into the arts where it is able to give a considerable amount of æsthetic pleasure.

The imaginative is more exclusively human. I have seen a large collection of photographs of tattooed women of New Guinea, and am told that the theory is that all the patterns, which are very beautiful and sometimes very complex, are believed to be derivations from imitative design. In some cases the patterns bear names of real objects, and a relationship can be traced between object and pattern; in others the derivation of the pattern is so remote that the name has become altered, or lost. This instinct for creating pattern from imitative drawing is worthy of more study. The New Guinea natives have long ago lost any perception of the bond between nature and their art; indeed, often it is not realized by them that the name of the pattern and the name of the natural object is the same word. At one time their bodies may have been pictograph poems instead of as to-day poems of abstract pattern. This phenomenon occurs all over the world. To those who can read it the Persian carpet is

74

almost as explicit as a Chinese manuscript, which is itself an ideographic development from a pictograph script. In the same way the hieratic script of Egypt was developed, and many of our own letters are derived from imitative drawings used as symbols.

Humanity has the patterning instinct.

A well-known round game is called " Russian Scandal." One member of a circle tells a story to his neighbour, who passes it on to the next member, and so from mouth to mouth it goes round the circle until it returns to the original raconteur. The two versions are then compared. Astounding variations will be found to have originated. The resultant story may be quite other than the first. Every new set of people will give a different resultant. Save under the duress of each learning the story by rote, it seems impossible for the tale to make the tour of a number of people and return unaltered. An interesting psychological experiment could be made were each person to write down the story, not as he receives it, but as he passes it on. The birth and growth of variation could then be traced. The greatest variations would coincide either with the person of an excitable mentality, who would tend to elaborate and over-emphasize points which caught the fancy, or with the austere minds, which would prune and lop off, reducing the tale as much as possible to a bare skeleton. It would be found that whenever a good example of either of these two types of mind was present at that moment the story would tend to become beautiful. Once the story *as a whole* had been grasped by a player who was able to bring unity to it, either by elaboration and inclusion or by exclusion, the story would tend to become a work of art. Thus, if the circle were at all a large one the æsthetic variations would be found to fluctuate almost as much as the variations in fact.

A similar experiment could be carried out in drawing, supposing a circle as adept in the use of the pencil as the average person is with words. But it is not necessary to experiment with Russian Scandal or its graphic equivalent. This game has been played all through the æons of man's existence. All the legends of the past have been developed in this way; most of the patterns have been evolved thus.

To return to the tattooing. The design may start, let us say, as a fairly accurate rendering of the Frigate-bird (Aurea). Once the original design is set, subsequent artists tend to copy the design rather than to go back to nature. Under successive copying the design " develops " farther and farther from nature, and tends to become more and more " pattern." This impulse is not confined to one part of humanity, but is almost universal. If under this continual copying and consequent slow change the life were gradually to ooze from the design, if it were to grow clumsy, uninteresting and dull, then with truth " degeneration " could be claimed. But this is not the case. The drawing does lose the beauty of imitation—rapidly—but it acquires a new beauty, that of design. This latter beauty is a beauty of art alone.

If the most profound impulse of humanity were towards realism, towards imitation of nature, successive genius would be continually at work regenerating pattern back to nature. There would result a sort of see-saw, the easy careless artistic kind of workmen debasing the work through slovenly copying, the great and real artists drawing it back to realism. In practice this does not occur. It is true that careless artists debase the pattern, and that the good artists revivify it, but this process of revivification is not through a return to nature, but usually by means of reasserting the value of proportion, space and rhythmic harmony. Like the tale in Russian Scandal we will find some good artists who make elaborations and complexities, while others strip down to the bare bones of structure. The one aims at the Beautiful, the other at the Sublime. But this process of revivification sometimes even helps to carry the pattern yet farther from nature. And towards nature no tendency to return is shown by instinct. A return to nature is always conscious. When, however, a partial return to nature is shown—and it occurs from time to time—it will usually be found to be coincident with a general decadence; when the moving spirit which dictated the major outline of the art is no longer a living force, when faith is dead, and when humanity has unconsciously to find some other background and a new reason for its art. In periods of decadence, complexity for the sake of complexity and a return to nature are almost inevitable.

As in the scandal game, a new set of players would evolve a different variation of the tale; so in pattern making from nature the designs evolved from any one natural object are unlimited in number and scope. But in the game only one medium is employed, the spoken word; in plastic art the variety of mediums used introduce a new reason for variation in development. The growth of design or of pattern will be found to be different in each material for which it is employed. That is to say, from the same natural object, the pattern or design evolved for wood, stone, tile, vase or textile would tend to become more and more differentiated. The growth of every pattern is thus dictated not solely by the will or genius of the artist, but by the quality of the medium. To more than a small extent beauty of design is enshrined in suitability, in a proper respect for the artistic medium employed. Thus, large works in stone must be more compact than large works in bronze, since stone is more breakable; and from this comes the fact that many of the broken fragments of Greek statuary are more beautiful than the completed figures, the processes of nature having reduced the work until it is suitable to its material.

When we speak of " pattern " we are using it in the broadest sense; it includes design, the organization of picture making, or composition. This impulse to pattern, as we have shown, is antagonistic to the reproduction of nature. The more design is pushed to ideal limits the more nature has to suffer. Picture making, which is representative, is essentially a compromise between these two. It combines the æsthetic (pattern) and scientific (imitative or analytic) aspects within the art of painting.

Science is the apotheosis of curiosity. It is true that Science is of immense benefit to humanity, but these benefits are by-products, and the true scientist is somewhat scornful of the secondary scientist who turns the solution of an absorbing problem into practical value. The scientist wishes to analyse and to make evident. The artist who is *primarily* interested in the representation of nature is a scientist at heart, he is an extrovert : he, too, wishes to analyse, to make clear. Science advances. A discovery in science remains a discovery. If it is a true discovery nothing can invalidate it. The atomic theory is not invalid because there are electrons, the atom remains the smallest individual part of recognizable matter which can exist. There is no need to go over the ground once more to make re-discoveries, and a discovery once made is at the service of any one who has sufficient learning to make use of it. The power of imitating natural shapes on a smaller scale in clay or bone was probably the first discovery which led to the evolution of the *outline*. Both of these are part æsthetic, part scientific, but once the properties of the outline are discovered there is no need of rediscovery. Colour as a representative factor follows much later. Perspective is hinted at in Assyrian monuments in which figures are placed higher and made smaller to indicate distance. This, however, is confused with the psychological custom (primarily æsthetic) of making figures smaller or larger to indicate their comparative life importances. Apelles, in Greece, is said to be the first to introduce perspective into Grecian painting and has been accused of being the leader of a decadence from Æsthetic to Scientific art. But perspective proper does not gain any firm hold till the Renaissance. Uccello illustrates both the stimulus and the danger of a new scientific discovery in art. Uccello was obsessed by perspective. His canvases are almost a treatise upon the science. Because his enthusiasm was roused so high by the science, his canvases became organized lyrics on perspective. But sometimes he introduces jarring elements, only to show his mastery over the craft. Once discovered perspective can be taught ; anyone with a foot-rule and a little application can become a master of perspective. It is imagined by some that European Art is superior to Japanese because the latter refuse to admit true perspective, without taking into consideration the fact that the so-called *true* European perspective is itself a convention and is in fact untrue to nature. If art does depend upon such a minor mechanical process as this it must be valueless indeed. Chiaroscuro and anatomy also belong to the Renaissance. Indeed, the Renaissance shows how quickly the general principles of Realism or of Scientific art are mastered if the mind turns in that direction. It is absurd to imagine that the great genius which created the Egyptian, the Byzantine, or the Gothic could not have worked realistically had it been so minded. The Chinese and Japanese definitely considered realism vulgar. The Egyptians reserved it for small ornaments or for death figures in which religious superstition demanded realism ; and when this was aimed at it was superbly achieved. There are few sculptures of the present day which can vie for vividness of presentation with the " Lady Nophret " in the Cairo Museum. In the Renaissance Leonardo da Vinci hints at the discoveries of Impressionism, but rejects them as valueless for art. From the time of Veronese scientific discovery almost halts until the colour analysis of light, hinted at by Turner, Constable, and Delacroix, was developed by the Impressionists.

These scientific discoveries have in themselves little value, and no necessary artistic worth. A work may be conventionally accurate in silhouette (outline) or in perspective or in anatomy, or the principles of Impressionism may be properly used, and no artistic results be arrived at. Each of the properties can be measured almost mathematically, and the first three can be produced by means of a machine such as the camera lucida, yet we come no closer to a work of art. The colour cinematograph has analysed light.

With the Impressionists (or their immediate followers, the Neo-Impressionists) the scientific analysis of nature comes to an abrupt stop. We cannot imagine any further valuable objective visual discoveries.

It is, therefore, noteworthy that at this exact moment painting takes a sudden leap away from imitation. The problem of realism is exhausted and instinctively art revolts from realism.

Art has always demanded a stimulus. Either it has come from religion, as in Europe, or from an internal sense of nature, as in China, or worship of the human body, as in Greece; and there is no doubt that since the decay of the religious impulse (Renaissance pictures are not primarily religious) the driving force in Europe has been scientific discovery. But the scientific analysis of vision (objective vision) has been exhausted. Artists cannot any longer excite themselves over the problems of how to reflect nature in paint; and, even had the camera not been invented, the practical solution of the problems of appearance are sufficiently complete.

The solution of the problem of design and the patterning instinct can never be completed. Every problem presented is a new problem. There are no instruments, no mechanical appliances to use for elucidation. The organization of colour, of design into an unison, the creation of space sensation, the communication of a mood by means of these forms and harmonies are problems which differ with each new approach and which only the immediate solution by the artist satisfies. There is no receipt in painting. For every new work the ingredients must perforce be different. In this the older artists were more courageous in some ways than our moderns; they were not afraid of borrowing one another's themes and reworking them; for under the new attack the result comes out fresh and renewed.

I have heard an attempted explanation of Modern Art which claims that it is work of an experimental nature. I think it is clear what is meant. The implication is that the experiment has not been successful. This is misleading. All art is of an experimental nature. The only work of no value is that which is not experimental. When the artist has his methods so arranged that he can use them mechanically, with the precision of a machine—without experiment—that art is bad. All great art is experimental, and the value of a work may be almost judged by the depth of the experiment attempted in it.

We can understand more clearly the value of experiment if we map out the career of the mediocre artist who has achieved one success. As a rule we find a period during which he is striving towards an aim. He emerges from his studenthood still struggling with the problems of his art, his work is experimental, and is not without interests. Gradually, but not without more experiment, he acquires skill. He, at length, paints the work which gains general recognition. The following years are devoted not to new experiment, but to consolidating the craft which he has gained, to ensure for himself the power to produce at will a repetition of his success. He wishes to make sure of the experimentalization by which he touched notoriety. From this onwards his art declines into repetition of the *means* by which he attained his climax ; but as he never attempts to repeat the conditions (*i.e.* experiment) he gradually loses what he had. Such is the career of any of the numerous artists of one fortunate picture, or that of the writers of one successful book. They fail because their success had daunted them from further experiment.

Herein we may note one of the chief dangers of a civilization of comfort, such as is our own : the decay of the love of adventure, the active fear of failure. The greatest things of life are reserved for the adventurous. There are adventures in thought no less exciting and no less dangerous than adventures in the physical. Every advance in culture has been made by the adventurous, and with the death of adventure comes the decay of culture. Therefore, if only for self-protection, humanity should encourage the adventurous. Every kind of adventure should be applauded. If the results of it are valueless the future generations will judge them : posterity can always be left to deal with results ; but for humanity the encouragement of even futile adventure will have a real value ; amongst the futile must also spring up the real.

When Gray says that in his lonely churchyard is buried

G

" perhaps some mute inglorious Milton," it is clear that this muteness and lack of glory are due to deficiency in the sense of adventure.

But to-day we do not honour the adventure. Indeed, the very word " adventurer " is made one of reproach. The whole training in our schools is to suppress the natural love of the unexperienced which struggles in the heart of man. To-day the rewards of this life are counted in comfort and respectability. These are the only rewards envisaged by comfortable and respectable parents. They do not understand that life contains other things. To the adventurous adventure is its own reward. And herein the comfortable public misjudge the artist; unadventurous, it can see no other recompense than riches or fame. But to the true artist riches and fame are but by-products. His reward is in the adventure, and for the sake of the adventure he accepts—and often receives—neglect, contempt and ridicule.

We have a theory of eugenics which is directed to the ideal of a healthy race, but more important still should be a conscious recognition of the adventurous which ensures a healthy civilization.

Experimentalization in art is not, however, of a scientific nature. A scientific experiment is one which elucidates and makes clear to everybody. Once the intelligence has grasped the intention and the method, anyone can judge whether the experiment has succeeded or no. Once understood, the experiment can be repeated. It is not necessary for the demonstrator to have the same genius as the discoverer. But in the experiments of art these conditions are not paralleled. No amount of intelligence will empower us to judge of the rightness or wrongness of a work of art. We may *understand* the principles employed and yet our sensibilities may fail to react. A work of art which has the power of operating only upon two or three persons, if it operates strongly enough, is a great work; for the value of art cannot be measured by the extent of its audience, but by the quality of emotion which it produces in its most responsive spectator.

When we contrast the scientific spirit with the creative we

HENRI MATISSE
THE MUSICIANS

realize that science is at root an extension of the monkey habit ; curiosity is strongly marked in animals, as is also the imitative element. One does not deny to science a creative element, nor does one deny an æsthetic content in scientific work. But the moving spirit behind science is curiosity ; analysis, not creation. This is but an extension of the animal. Creation is human. Art and not science most profoundly marks our separation from the rest of the animal world.

Matisse comes in as a prime example of the adventurous man, with a sense of pattern. He is the first of that important group of artists who developed from the leadership of Cézanne, Van Gogh, Gauguin and Renoir. Yet although considering Matisse (around whom, with Picasso, controversy has raged more furiously than around the others) we cannot feel that he, along with the other disciples and leaders of to-day, had quite the same vital impulse as that which drove Van Gogh, Cézanne or Seurat into the routes which they had chosen. These latter men were pioneers, they plunged out boldly to explore a country which everybody else believed to be but a mirage. They brought back evidences which few would believe. Matisse, Derain, Picasso, Bracque and the rest are the believers who set out to map and to cultivate the terrain discovered by others. But their genius *as discoverers* is of a lower order, they have not quite the same sense of adventure as their predecessors. They are related to Cortés rather than to Columbus.

We come here to the fact that artists can be divided into two classes. The creative impulse can develop from two centres : either the artist has a spiritual driving force, which compels him to find a means of expression, or else he is greatly gifted with craft, and has to struggle to find some motive upon which to work. El Greco and Blake are examples of the first ; Holbein, Veronese or Tiepolo are examples of the second. The first kind of artist may fail for two reasons : either he is not able to learn or invent a craft strong enough to express his aims, or else the consciousness of the public is not sufficiently sensitive, or is too prejudiced, to receive his message—the genius of Blake is still but partially admitted, and El Greco was successful because of the *naïveté* of his Spanish audience. Had El Greco tried to paint sixty years ago he would have been worse received than was Cézanne. Doubtless many men of great artistic possibilities have been lost to the world in this way, condemned to muteness by a lack of executive skill, or rejected because unintelligible, or more possibly burned as wizards or ostracized as revolutionaries. This artist may be placed in a type which we will call A.

The artist of the other type—type B—usually avoids serious contemporary contretemps. He is first of all the embodiment of supreme skill. His intellectual ideas are not an obsession for him as they are for the other man. If he has real artistic sensibility, he gathers enough inner fire to himself to make his pictures of permanent value. With him the struggle is never how to say, but what to say. Out of this species comes the great body of artistic produce, and when the skill is supreme without intelligence one gets the Guido Renis, the Murillos, the Canovas and the Millais. If we go back to consider these two classes of artists as indicators of social conditions, we may compare them to two classes of thermometer. There is one kind of thermometer which will record sensation of heat produced by a fire a mile away. Such a thermometer responds to a change of temperature long before it has become humanly sensible; the other common garden thermometer only measures our physical sensations; to conflagrations two miles off it is supremely indifferent.

The mental difference between these two classes of artists is that he of the A type is always conscious of his lack of executive skill. He is always stretching out, straining the limits of his powers to cracking point. As Mr. Berenson points out, such an artist is always talking about technique, because that is just what worries him; and, although fundamentally he is antagonistic to the idea that art is technique, he helps more than any other to make the public believe that supreme art is supreme technical achievement. He

BONNARD
A WOMAN INDOORS

thus really antagonizes the public to his own aim and concentrates the attention upon the works of the artists of the B type. The painter of this latter order is rarely conscious of his lack of intelligence. He trusts to, and rejoices in, his skill alone.

Suddenly we get a third class of artist who is produced by the novel conditions. This class of artist might be compared to a garden thermometer, which becomes aware of the distant conflagration and struggles to record its faint radiant heat. This class of artist is a group drawn from persons of the B type, who perceive that technique is not the sole aim of art. These artists realize that technique is but a body to which the soul gives life. They realize that in themselves the soul struggles hampered by this body of technique. One must imagine a converted Falstaff struggling to escape from his mental and bodily corpulence. He would come to hate his fat as something degrading to his aspiring soul. The phenomenon has been exhibited in a thousand variations since the birth of Christianity. To-day we have a similar thing in art. Matisse may be considered as a converted Falstaff. A pupil of the Beaux Arts and subsequently employed by the French government to copy the old masters from the Louvre, Matisse has given many a proof of a technical ability high even according to the standards of his most furious adversaries. But I think it is clear that without Van Gogh and Gauguin there might have been no Matisse. Yet we must not take our two classes as being entirely independent. There is no such thing as a hard edge in nature, even the razor under the microscope betrays its shortcomings. In life the hero is one-third villain and the villain one-third of a hero.

Matisse, in reality, shocked his audience not because he knows too little, but because he knows too much ; not because he cannot draw, but because he has learned exactly how much drawing is worth. He was almost too logical. His earlier pictures seem not so much the direct result of sensation, of an emotion remembered in tranquillity, as of an emotion reconstructed in moments of logical activity. Matisse was the leader of a school which distrusted its own ability. It realized painfully how extreme brilliance too often is but reflected light, as in a diamond, not an evidence of real internal fire. To get at those qualities of the first order, which lie within itself, it ruthlessly tramples upon qualities of the second order, which alone would have been sufficient to gain for it reward as an academic painter. To keep alive the spirit it mortifies the flesh.

The supreme personal gift of Matisse is colour. But colour alone means nothing. He takes his colour out of the same tubes as any other painter. These exquisite blues, these acid greens, these astonishing pinks are normal painters' colours, but his gift of setting them together brings from each new and vivid qualities which had hitherto lain dormant waiting for the magic prince to awaken them. "Colour," says Aristotle, "may mutually relate like musical concords for their pleasantest arrangement: like those concords mutually proportionate."

Aristotle had that uncanny perception which so often illuminated the Greek thinkers (the intuitive perception of the atom amongst other scientific *discoveries* of recent times). Colour does mutually relate like musical concords, but the European painters obsessed by realism had, on the whole, failed to perceive the importance of this fact. The great colourists, such as Titian or Fra Angelico, or Watteau, imposed their colour schemes on nature by an instinct; but were often limited in the resources of their magnificence. Like poor kings they often had but one or two robes of ceremony.

It is possible, indeed, that colour vision has developed mentally if not physically. There is a theory that the Greeks did not *see* blue, and this theory is substantiated by the fact that the South American natives have only two colour perceptions, white and chestnut. To these peoples all colours which are light are white, all dark are chestnut. They cannot naturally distinguish between blue and red of the same depth of colour. But this vision can be trained to perceive colours; this relates to that brain inhibition of vision of which we spoke in a previous chapter.

Be the reason what it may, colour vision in painting has been

HENRI MATISSE
THE YOUNG SAILOR. (1906)

on the whole, low compared with the progress in other branches. Monet was the first conscious colourist, and he gives place to Signac. Cézanne developed a colour vision of his own, for his own purposes, and in his water-colours we see a complete suppression of *local* colour in order that he may use colour to reinforce his sense of space : yellows used to bring things forward, blues and violets to push them back, and so on. Van Gogh used colour emotionally—red to express warmth; orange, lovableness; blue, coldness and remoteness. Gauguin uses colour barbarically, for the sheer exuberance of pure tint.

It remained, however, for Matisse to carry the use of pure colour to a pitch which has hitherto had few rivals. The pictures of Matisse's middle period are shaped in pure tints or clean greys, which are a delight to the chromatically sensitive onlooker. He achieves that most difficult task, a high quality of unexpectedness in colour combined with variety. He does not play on one or two notes as do so many painters, who are content to rely for the rest of their days upon a few chance and happy discoveries of their youth. He has used colour as a musical composer uses chords, as deliberately chosen and definite harmonic progressions.

But though Matisse's great *personal* gift is his colour vision, the chief service which he has rendered to painting lies in his drawing. We perceive in Matisse's early work the hesitation and instinctive gropings after other men's formulæ, which mark the dawning consciousness in the artist of Class B of the shortcomings of his natural outlook. Impressionism had produced two men who were not Impressionists at all save in superficial appearance. These two are Bonnard and Vuillard. With that craze for plunging painters into categories of " isms " which mean nothing at all, these two painters have been harnessed together with the sobriquet of " Intimists." It is safer to throw most recent " isms " out of the window. At the beginning, the word Cubism had some meaning, although it was invented in derision by Matisse ; but the subsequent crop of Orphists, Futurists, Synchromists, Purists, Simultaneists,

Dada-ists and so on, are as a rule irritating adjectives with no real meaning which often sheltered the all-pervading " ist," the arrivist, the self-advertiser, the get on or get out painter who has been the curse of modern art.   Bonnard and Vuillard derive a general technique from the Impressionists ; but their colour is personal and delicate and they both show a natural sense of design, which often combines the flow of Renoir with the unexpectedness of Degas.

Matisse in his first tentative experiments away from the Artistes Français arrived at a sort of rigid compromise between Academism and Bonnardism.   But once he became fully aware of the real object of his search he went rapidly forward, with but a short digression into Pointillism which gave no satisfaction to his apparently impatient character.

Matisse had been one of the most persistent of experimentalists amongst the painters of to-day, but he has known how to control his experiments within a limited field.   He has been but little influenced by changing fashion, and more than any other artist of to-day has logically followed his own development.   Matisse's experiments have been directed towards a research for simplification of drawing and a rapidity of the statement, a sort of short-hand of what is taking place in the mind.   This drawing often becomes arbitrary, but is almost always harmonious and living. The sense of space is suggested by colour oppositions and subtly used contrasts rather than by modelling, which Matisse is only to-day introducing into his work.

Matisse has been called the chief of the " Fauves " ; * his pictures have aroused wild orgies of reprobation.   He was accused of throwing painting into chaos and disorder.   Yet, if anything, upon analysis, his pictures are but too logical.   One sometimes finds a composition which almost offends because it is so obvious, such as the portrait of M. Pellerin.   The linear design tends to lack magic because it is explained too completely.

The work of Matisse brought a precision of its own into the

* Wild beasts.

MARQUET
LA ROCHELLE, (1920)

quality of drawing in modern painting. At the moment when he began to reveal his gifts, painting in general was under the influence of the Impressionists and Pointillists : it tended amongst the lesser disciples towards either vagueness or vulgarity. Cézanne had scarcely yet been understood; Henri Rousseau was so much the butt of the Independents that the hanging committee after hiding his pictures in a dark corner would soak the floor with pools of water in order to prevent the jeering crowds from gathering before his naïve images. Valloton was perhaps the only painter who pursued a cold research with uncompromising definition of drawing. Both Gauguin and Van Gogh were still suspect, and in 1900, the year before Matisse first exhibited in the Salon des Indépendants, an important Seurat was sold in a public auction for twenty-seven francs ; it would now be worth fifty or sixty thousand.

At the same time as Matisse, Marquet, developing from Renoir into a simplicity of his own seeking, began to bring into the painting of landscape a simplification of realistic drawing which has had a very considerable effect upon the younger painters, especially upon Derain, Braque, and upon Matisse himself. In contrast with Matisse, who pushed colour farther and farther towards the extremes of contrast, Marquet's palette sobers towards diluted tints, which in later years become dangerously near to the unpleasant quality of those in the oleographic print. Matisse's drawing is swift and tends to subject itself to the natural sweeps of the hand ; Marquet's is rigid and resolves easily into angularity. There is thus a difference between these two painters of a nature somewhat similar to that between Renoir and Cézanne.

Rouault is a sort of hermit, *un insolite,* amongst the modern art of to-day. A man who by his art could have raised as much controversy as Matisse, who could have had as much influence as Derain, he has followed his own path, keeping quietly clear both of limelight and of controversy.

Rouault has, perhaps, had no followers. He has completed his art so fully that *following* in the true sense of the word is impossible. One can follow Cézanne, for Cézanne has opened up a wide horizon to which one can trace one's own path. But Renoir and Rouault complete quite definite aspects of a general artistic theory. One can learn from Renoir's subtle composition of movement, one can appreciate his use of spherical volumes, and from this knowledge one can add to one's own powers. But one must use these in one's own way, one cannot step off from Renoir's shoulders. In a similar way one can learn from Rouault's passion, one can fortify oneself with the almost crude vitality of his work, but one cannot develop from him. To develop from Rouault would be to do Rouault over again. He is not a road, but an impasse.

This is of course the natural result of an artist who insists upon personality ; he becomes inimitable. One could copy Fielding, but one cannot copy Sterne. Rouault develops directly from his training as a craftsman in stained glass. His pictures have the illumination of transparencies, but his drawing, especially of late, is brutal, as though dictated by leaden limitations. He takes his place as a painter in the group which encloses Van Gogh and Vlaminck. If Marquet is the eye, Rouault is the heart of his epoch. He is a painter essentially of the A nature. His methods of expression are merely the natural result of what he has to express. Thus, one finds in him none of the heart burnings and brain searchings of a Matisse, a Derain or a Picasso. Rouault paints *comme l'oiseau chante*, or rather, in view of his subjects and his attitude, he paints like a cabby swears.

ROUALT
BALLARINA

CHAPTER IX

HENRI ROUSSEAU AND UTRILLO

MATISSE, once accused of drawing like a five-year-old child, replied: "That is what I am trying to do, I should like to recapture that freshness of vision which is characteristic of extreme youth, when all the world is new to it."

matisse

Here at once we see signs of the artist of the B type, who is aware that something of the spontaneous vision of type A has been lost by him; that, in fact, something foreign has been imposed on his personal sense of external nature; to which he struggles to return by thinking himself back to his early childhood, to the time before this imposition was begun.

The worn-out phrase, the threadbare convention of the journalist, the locution which merely serves to save the writer from having to construct his own thoughts into an image, has long been condemned in literature. Phrases such as " muffled curses," " she cast down her eyes," " sleeping the sleep of the just," etc., etc., are recognized as a method of writing adopted only by the slovenly artist. The same is true of the painter. If we could have a royal school of journalism, one part of its duties would probably be that of collecting all such phrases, which the pupils would be trained to memorize so that they should be ready for any occasion. This is practically what the art school is doing. It strives to make the student an unconscious user of the ideas and mannerisms of other men. The viciousness of the system is evident to the person who is trying to put his thoughts clearly and in his own way. Constantly, ready to his hand, rush out

91

these trite and outworn phrases, and often indeed he employs them almost unaware that he is using a mouldy phrase and that by doing so he has but clouded his meaning.

Matisse in his early work gives the example of a man who becomes aware that much of his vocabulary is journalism. To cure himself of this acquired impediment he goes back to the language of childhood. Technically in this respect one may compare his works to Maeterlinck's plays or Wilde's " Salome " ; he paints in short and pregnant sentences, having perceived that the short sentence is more easy to control, and that complexity is not necessary to produce works of art. At this moment appears another figure who is the antithesis to Matisse, just as Van Gogh is the antithesis to Cézanne. Henri Rousseau was an employé in the French Excise, and only took seriously to painting upon his retirement from the service, and though he had worked for years he only began to gain recognition at about the time that Matisse began his own development. Matisse was a painter who conceived a terror of painting in a trite way, while Rousseau's desire was to paint a picture so conventional that he would be admitted to the Artiste Français. If he lacked a detail for some portion of his picture, he used to go to the Louvre, where he searched amongst the Old Masters until he discovered some object which he considered suitable to his own work. He then memorized this and went home to put it into his own canvas. Thus, we see that while Matisse was shunning triteness Rousseau was deliberately seeking it. Rousseau is like a man of original literary talent who is struggling to drag his natural language down to the level of that of a provincial paper. He did not succeed because the clichés which he tried to memorize escaped him, automatically substituting in the place something which was natural to his peculiar genius.

I have showed that the statement " we learn to see through pictures " contains a great deal of the truth, that, though we actually have a vision of nature, the things of which we see clearly are learned from pictures and drawings of them. Yet even the untutored, those who have seen no pictures, have more than a mere notion of

HENRI ROUSSEAU

THE QUARRY

what they are looking at ; as also those peasants who live far from books yet have an idea of diction, poetry, and beauty of speech. Every country has its body of folk-lore and that folk-lore can be no better presented than in the very speech, uncultivated though it may be, in which it was invented. It is true that most of the attempts to resurrect the beauties of dialect are of an artificial nature, Burns being, perhaps, the outstanding exception. Yet, if one can remember the beauties of the dialect which one heard in one's childhood, one cannot but be saddened that those mute inglorious Miltons (if they existed) did not leave more traces of their bar-parlour improvisations in a country tongue. It is certain that if one of these lost improvisers had come across some phrases of superb journalism he would possibly have tried to incorporate them into his art, with much the effect of a top hat clapped on to the head of a cannibal emperor. Another aspect of dialect to make clear our thesis upon Henri Rousseau is that dialect changes less rapidly than polite speech. There are still parts of England where Chaucer would be more comprehensible than Browning. It is only in recent years that folk-lore and folk music have received any serious attention from artistes ; and the equivalent in painting has received none at all. This is to some extent due to that conjunction of painting and luxury of which we have made mention before ; which has not weighed so heavily upon the sister arts of music and literature. The great body of dialect art which has been produced in literature must be suspect, for the poet must become writer, that is, must gain some practical acquaintance with the polite speech before he is able to leave a record of his poems. Exceptions to this rule, however, may be found in more primitive countries than our own—in the ancient war ballads of Serbia, or the popular coplas of Spain. Music, however, is a more natural art. If you have a traditional instrument, no learning other than finger practice is necessary to him who would produce melodies, and these melodies become naturally interchanged between players and so are preserved. Thus the balalaika music of Russia, the guitar music of Spain, the cobla music of Catalonia, and the bagpipe music of Scotland have been evolved without any aid or interference from musicians with an academic training.

Folk painting has received little encouragement. The icons and popular prints of Russia are worthy of mention, for they form almost the sole example; but painting, like literature, has been held under the bar of scholarship, and the reproductions of pictures have, like books, been wafted down to the common herd from Olympian heights above.

As we see in Chaucer and Malory the traces of what we would to-day consider English or French Folk poetry, so in the early Italian primitive painters, and, indeed, in primitives of every order, we find beneath the artists' learning the foundations laid upon what may be called folk painting. The first attempt to recapture the charm of these works was made by the Pre-Raphaelites, and we may compare their attempts to those of the literary men who have gone out of their way to write in dialect. But it is an artificial attempt. Dialect is not the natural language of a learned literary man any more than Pre-Raphaelitism was the natural development for a learned painter who lived after Turner. The logical development for the Pre-Raphaelites was Impressionism, and over all their works, in spite of the talent often exhibited, hangs the veil of an affected mannerism which is irritating to the sensitive spectator.

In spite of the fact that painting has suffered more than any other art from the savant and the professor, it is a more natural art than any, save, perhaps, singing and dancing. The poet must learn how to write in metre, the instrumentalist how to accord his instrument. The artist has only to choose a flat stone and to stick his fingers into wet clay to produce drawings of the first quality, and as a proof of this there exist drawings and paintings in the caves of Spain which give evidence of an extraordinary high level of painting ability at a period (Magdelinian) when both speech and music must have been of a most primitive variety.

We have seen in an earlier chapter that an uninitiated man attempting to draw a bucket produces a figure which is part observation and part preconception. The painting has to include both vision

and knowledge, but the vision may be subordinated to the presentation of knowledge.   This painting is essentially descriptive painting.
It has its simplest expression in the drawings of the child, and when
the child is not content that it has clearly described the article in
drawing it adds a rubric—this is a tree—this is a dog, etc.   The
child who becomes a little more adept decorates his tree with large
green leaves, and his dog with a fluffy tail, and so can dispense with
the legend.   This kind of presentation is the presentation of an
object as it is understood by the brain, not as it is seen by the eye.
That is, it is a purely natural presentation, whereas the painter's
vision is of a specialized variety.   To the trained painter a bridge
is a mass in light and shadow, to the natural painter it is an erection
of blocks of stone.   When we think of a tree we do not picture a
green mass in light and shade, but we imagine a trunk which bursts
out into a corona of leaves, and we seldom think of a bridge without
mentally piling up the stones of its arches.

The artist who works in this way touches with a tender finger
the natural processes of the mind, though he may disturb the learned
processes of the vision.   Such a man was Henri Rousseau, the
douanier.   He is not seeking the strange, but the normal; he does
not try to show us what we do not know, but what everybody does
know.   But this normal is not quite the normal of *vision*, for vision
deals first with light and shade, afterwards with surface accidentals,
and lastly with construction.   Rousseau works inversely to this
rule.   He would not have been staggered by the visual artist's
impossible problem, a black man chasing a black cat in a black cellar
at midnight.

Writers have often used the device of putting profound and
sometimes paradoxical truths into the mouths of very simple people.
These truths are also found in popular proverbs, and have much of
their force because of the breadth of common sense and of hidden
meaning which lies wrapped up in an apparently banal truism.
It is said that the Chinese poet strives to condense his thoughts into
the smallest compass ; like the sage in " The Arabian Nights " who

gradually condensed and condensed his knowledge so that from a hundred volumes he brought down all his wisdom to one line of script. There is much of this condensed and simple wisdom in the paintings of Rousseau. These pictures of bourgeois wedding groups, and of *fêtes-champêtres* are records of what the bourgeois really enjoys. They are painted with the same satisfied seriousness as that with which Van Eyck painted the portrait of a merchant and his wife. Two centuries hence these pictures will be invaluable, because they are the only genuine serious record of French middle-class life which exist. All the others have been painted by superior artists with snobbery in their hearts.

Rousseau is the folk painter, and he has the aspirations of the peasant. He can perceive no greater joy and no higher honour than that of promotion to the ranks of the small *commerçant*. He expresses naïvely and pregnantly the aspirations of a whole class of society and gives the lie to the artist who would sentimentalize about the peasant. But though Rousseau's peculiar point of view gives an unwonted charm to his pictures, they are not works of art because he has of necessity to use the only means of expression possible to him. The would-be naïve does not further his art by adopting deliberately this method of representation. Some of Rousseau's charm depends upon his mentality, but the whole is wrapped up in his art. Expression and technique are so blended that we cannot detach his methods from his final result. Yet this final result does not depend upon method. To revert to a simile used in an earlier chapter, one must have the meat in order to make a dish. Once the meat is there the flavouring can be added.

Rousseau's art springs from a fresh, simple perception of life, and it shows itself in the ways proper to art. Not by an accurate representation of nature, but by a subconscious organization of nature's effects to create harmonies of colour and of form. Because his perceptions are more simple than those of ordinary painters, his harmonies often depart widely from those of conventional art.

There is one artist whom we can place as a parallel with Rousseau,

HENRI ROUSSEAU
THE GIRL IN THE WOOD

for although he does not imitate the Douanier yet his art appeals through a similar channel and he may be considered as a genuine development of that folk-art of which Rousseau is the finest exponent. This painter is Utrillo.

The result of a use of mental realities—instead of carefully studied aspects—to produce artistic effect, is that the artist may with them more powerfully create the *genius loci* of his object. We do not, as a rule, remember things which are fugitive as easily as those which are permanent. Thus, a landscape such as that in the background of Piero della Francesca's " Nativity " recalls the actual quality of Southern Europe more forcibly than does either Corot or Turner. The latter artists are often only interested in a study of light effects, in an analysis of nature's appearance at a particular moment. Therefore, if we do not catch her again at such a moment something has gone out of the likeness. But Piero is concerned with the placing of two or three trees upon the side of a hill over a particular kind of stream. These features are recognizable no matter what light may play over the object.

All primitive art, because it deals with mental symbols, has this vivid power of awakening belief. We are more ready to credit the Angels of Fra Angelico than those of Veronese; Botticelli's goddesses are more divine than those of Rubens.

Utrillo, however, is not the natural bourgeois that was Rousseau, for it is almost unbelievable that Rousseau lived in nineteenth-century Paris. In consequence, though Utrillo shares with the Douanier a common freshness of vision and of method, his actual technique is very different. He is, however, the urban equivalent to Rousseau. He has a simplicity which has attracted itself to the streets which he paints with so much love and care. It is a part of the inherently romantic nature of modern man that he has refused to accept the town as matter for art. If he must paint the town at all, he chooses either some corner made romantic by associations or else he veils the bricks and mortar with a curtain of atmospheric effect. Utrillo accepts bricks and mortar. He accepts everything that the town

H

has to give, and creates thus a vision of Paris of which the most remarkable part is that nobody had noted it before. It is extraordinary how often the obvious is the most difficult to perceive.

We can note both in the work of Utrillo and in that of Rousseau more than a hint of that olden simplicity which we call primitiveness, and which is so prominent in folk-lore. It would seem, indeed, as though we are contradicting the very statements that we made in Chapter VII., where we showed that art must go forwards imposing itself upon nature because man is doing so. But this imposition of which we spoke is a thing of various degrees. As the hero is often as much villain, so this civilization is a mixture of the new and of the old. We are yet in the final stage of evolution. The Gothic peasant does not lie far below the skin of the bourgeois, who to-day takes flying-machines and drains for granted. This is the order that Rousseau represents.

It would be too much to state that all Rousseau's works or all of Utrillo's are of the first order. Indeed no artist is always a genius. *Nemo omnibus horis sapit.* But when Rousseau and Utrillo are good they have a genius and a quality, a subdued richness and a simplicity which are a never-failing source of delight.

UTRILLO

A SUBURBAN STREET

CHAPTER X

SAVAGE ART AND MODIGLIANI

BECAUSE he is dead and his work therefore complete, we will treat Modigliani anterior to his proper place before we treat of those still living. In reality he comes after the period represented by Derain, Dufy, Friesz, Vlaminck and others which began to be marked about 1900. We will treat Modigliani earlier for another reason ; his work illustrates the entry of certain forces which had a great influence upon the Independents, influences which we can treat through Modigliani because in him they show their traces the most clearly.

From Leonardo until the Impressionists the only ancient art which had any general recognition was the art of Greece, and, within architectural limits only, the art of the Gothic. During Napoleon's day that gigantic masterpiece of Egyptian culture, the Sphinx, was massacred by the soldiery of the " most intelligent nation of Europe." It was, however, almost an accident that this Greek art became the ideal of the Renaissance. The art of Fra Angelico, of Botticelli and of the French Primitives indicates a line upon which the arts of Europe might have developed, had ancient Greece and imperial Rome been a little more effectively obliterated by the Turks or by the Goths. This art was in principal an architectural and a coloured art rather than an attempt at naturalistic imitation. It was an art which depended upon spirit rather than upon material, thus fulfilling the first law of the Chinese artistic canon, " Ch'i yun shen tung," which has been translated as " Spiritual rhythm expressed in the movement of life." But this art was turned into the materialistic development which reaches a climax with Veronese and Frans Hals.

99

The Impressionists, Cézanne, Van Gogh and Gauguin, aimed a blow at the prestige of Greek art. Though Greek art reached a perfection in certain directions, it was seen that these directions had their limits. Greek art often appears better after rough nature had done some sculpture upon it ; for instance, the Venus de Milo has been greatly improved by the loss of her arms. As the supremacy of Greek art began to be questioned, the virtues of the arts of other countries were examined, and the Chinese, the Egyptian, the Gothic, the Byzantine and the Persian revealed their peculiar and unique beauties, which in many directions pass beyond the Greek. Both Van Gogh and Gauguin were strongly influenced by these Oriental arts. The West was getting ready to receive ideas about the aspects of things which have for long been commonplaces in the East. But all these arts were complex and complete systems. They corresponded to highly developed civilizations and were in consequence themselves highly developed ; and, since highly developed civilization is highly artificial, the arts were as artificial. This artificiality prevented these arts from becoming direct models for new productions. The lessons which they could teach could be learned ; but the actual forms were too complete as art to be employed again. They *belonged* to other cultures.

However, Gauguin, in his search for a primitive life, went to the Marquesas, and attention was turned towards an order of art quite different from those of which we have been speaking. This art was the product of civilizations the simplest known ; save, perhaps, those of the bushmen and the Eskimos. It is the result of the most primitive conditions which are capable of producing finished art. This was the civilization of the African negro. We have seen that Matisse wished to think himself back to five years old in order to free himself from the commonplaces and inhibitions of a past era. A similar result can be obtained by studying the art of a simple people. Such an art is a simple and instinctive thing, and tends to keep clear those impulses which drove the artist to original creation.

There is another art which might have had an influence at this time, had it been known. This art was that of the Southern Spanish paleolithic cave-dwellers. But the principle of this art—which has only been revealed recently and which is still practically unknown— in the essentials have now been worked out by modern artists themselves and what might have been revelation twenty-five years ago is common knowledge nowadays. There are also a number of minor civilizations which have contributed to the growing consciousness of the importance of design, the power of the fundamental qualities of painting over the surface qualities of realism, notably Peruvian art and American-Indian art, both of which are bold and successful in their departures from nature in obedience to demands of design. But that art which at this moment contributed to the modern developments was the art of the negro.

Cézanne had shown the importance of structural composition and of the design of recession in painting. Renoir had created rhythmical and sweeping linear compositions which enclosed solid forms; Van Gogh had given rein to the mad fury of his imagination; Matisse had freed drawing from all triviality, and had demonstrated how expressive a simple line could become. All these qualities are present in Negro art as powerfully as it is possible to imagine it in any art. The Negro art concentrates in general upon the idea of creating images of mystic import in harmony with the religion of " Tabu." As we noted in reference to the tattoo patterns of New Guinea, the designing instinct of man here again is allowed freedom. The representation of humanity is more and more conventionalized, more and more simplified and withdrawn from realism. We find images of extraordinary power, full of subconscious suggestion, amongst these carvings. They solve in the simplest and frankest way many of the problems confronting the artist of to-day; yet in spite of this simplicity they convey to the fullest extent the effect intended. These masks of War Gods or of Devil Dancers convey their meaning in a more powerful and more direct manner than all the tortured humanity of the naturalistic European school.

These sculptures in wood reveal what are called *plastic* qualities of the highest order, that is to say, their virtues lie in their shapes, in the curves and in the contrasts of their surfaces. They are the works of men who have thought only as sculptors; there is no literary preconstruction. Sometimes these images become so conventionalized that all semblance to representation is lost, yet without a sacrifice of the meaning. They thus become *abstract* works of art, depending upon qualities which are those of painting alone, thus speaking the pure language of the painter's art, as music speaks with its own tongue, borrowing from no other art, nor requiring to be explicit in order to be intelligible.

This art had had a strong effect upon Derain, Dufy, Vlaminck, Picasso and, indeed, sub-consciously upon the whole younger school of painters. It remains, however, less prominently visible in the works of these painters than it does in the work of Modigliani. We have here an art neither romantic nor classic. It combines at once the precision and completeness which marks the classical and the suggestiveness which marks the Romantic.

Out of this primitive art Modigliani has built up a vision which is not primitive at all. He creates his figures in a convention which is modified from this negro sculpture, decorated with a colour the simplicity of which often is in exquisite harmony with the linear construction. He builds up a sense of solidity with the subtlest of tonality, sometimes analogous to that employed by his great countryman, Botticelli. With an art so simplified as this there is no middle path, no half success. Half success is failure, for there are no hazy passages in which the spectator can lose himself in dreams in order to create his own sentiment. Modigliani has faults : he repeats himself; his formula often becomes tiresome and strained. But in his best work he has a directness of statement, a clear vision, a grasp of form, and a power over subtle colour and the handling of his materials which, undoubtedly, give him a prominent place amongst the best painters of to-day. The series of caryatides which he has drawn with a pure pencil outline, afterwards simply

MODIGLIANI
PORTRAIT OF MME ZBOROWSKA

coloured with chalks, are, perhaps, the easiest method by which to appreciate what Modigliani was striving for.

The Negro art is an art of a static or of a stable nature. There is in it a sort of Yogi power, force emanating from quietude. But the pre-historic paintings of the late paleolithic races, especially those which have been discovered in the South of Spain, are analyses of pure movement. These paintings have already done what the Futurists were trying to do, and in a far simpler fashion. It seems at first a curious thing that these arts of primitive people reach to pitches of perfection which, in their way, have never been surpassed. We realize that art changes but does not progress. It seems like a polyhedron slowly turning ; we get different facets one after another, but the general shape does not alter. Art depends upon psychological and physiological peculiarities of man which lie far deeper than education or civilization. Indeed, the fact that primitive and primeval art can still move us is, in itself, a proof that art lies deeper than any education. Often the simpler nature can reach the quintessence of art more easily than the one which has been civilized, complicated and tangled with ideas extraneous to art itself.

CHAPTER XI

" SPACE " AND " LIFE " IN PAINTING

THE world is *seen* in colour alone. We have no sight but by means of colour. Light and shade, which give so strong a relief to objects, are merely more or less brilliance of reflected illumination. Pure white is intensity of illumination, pure black—which does not exist in nature—is total absence of colour. But light and shade are not a mere whitening or blackening of colour, but consist of a play of different colourings which often differ greatly from the nominal (or local) colour of the shaded object.

A second perception is inherent in the gift of sight, and is learned through the sense of colour, though in reality it is dissociated from this sense. This is the perception of space, or solidity. Space is partly muscular, partly visual. The young child makes " shots " at grasping an object and only gradually begins to associate sight and distance. The muscular focus of the eyes becomes associated with the sense of touch. Distances beyond the actual reach of the child are learned by a mental extension of the grasping powers. Some persons never co-ordinate perfectly vision and muscular effort. These we call clumsy.

It is necessary for comfortable existence that our understanding of space should be dissociated from plain sight. When we see an object, we view it from but one aspect at a moment. Let us consider a round polished mahogany table. From every different point of view both the visual shape and the colour appear to change. Yet we can say positively that the table is round ; although we never see it as round, but as a varied series of ovals ; and that it is of a brown colour, although we do not see its local (inherent) colour, the polish reflecting more or less distinctly all the objects in the room. It may even appear green in places, purple elsewhere, and, if we were to judge by vision alone, the table as we walk around it would seem to be undergoing a series of incredible changes.   But we never lose the certainty that the solidity and actual colour are positive and permanent.

Thus, our understanding of nature separates into two parts : first, the visual ; secondly, those permanencies which lie behind vision.   Both of these also divide into two, colour and space—or shape.

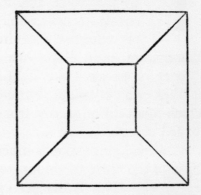

We have shown that paint cannot hope to rival the intensity of nature in colour ; and it is obvious that all space suggestions in painting are quite artificial, since a canvas has only length and breadth.

The painter wishes to make his space positive and give to it a definite reality which the spectator cannot ignore.   In the true presentation of space (as opposed to deception) we find that there is a mental conception of space, in which the optical sense is not disturbed to the point of illusion and the flat surface of the picture is not destroyed.   Sense of space combined with retention of surface is one of the most common of phenomena.

We can consider the above drawing as a flat pattern, as a truncated pyramid seen from above, or as a view through a long rectangular box.   By a small but quite perceptible mental juggle, we can make the diagram assume one phase after another; yet in no case is the eye deluded into the belief that the paper as surface is anything but flat.

Let us consider another figure less obviously illusive than the first.

Here again we can see the figure in three phases, but the associations which it has with the cube are so strong that the other phase of its appearance may be neglected. The sensation of the cubic nature of this diagram actually is more intense than that of a solid cube itself. In a real cube we are not tempted to concentrate upon this one quality of the cubic to the exclusion of other aspects. There the thing itself is before us ; our mind has become so accustomed to it as a concept formed from many associations that we pay little attention to it. Expressed, however, on the flat by nine

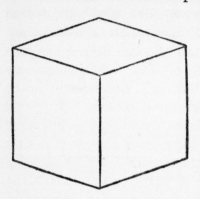

straight lines, the drawing becomes recognizable as a cube, because we concentrate upon the cubic relationship. When we lose grasp of this the figure reverts to a flat pattern. We thus, as it were, to comprehend the drawing, make a mental dissociation of the cubic from all the other natural properties of a cube, hardness, colour, light and shade, material, etc. And, because the figure becomes only cubic when we exert our senses upon this single property, we find that the cubic quality has acquired a more positive value. Thus, consciousness of space or solidity, when combined with a lack of actual space, makes us aware of an increase in our powers of perception, because, in order to become aware of the spatial (or solid) quality, we must concentrate upon it to the exclusion of any other impression.

If, however, the cube were so well imitated in paint that at a short distance we were unable to distinguish it from an actual cube, this mental dissociation of the cubic qualities would be no longer necessary. When we had lost the astonishment called up by the artist's dexterity (and this would in time die down) the painting would become as ordinary in relation to cubic (or spatial) values as the real cube ; we would at once lose the sense of the heightening of our perceptive powers. Thus, for the recognition of certain properties of objects the power of picturing without imitating results in a heightening of the consciousness. By this means art can make sensible to us even in small things that magic value of space which in nature we perceive only before the vista or in the cathedral.

We have said that there appears to be an inherent value in different plane figures—the circle, the oval, the curve, the angle, etc. —the emotional value of which seems to vary in some ratio with the muscular excitement caused by the figure, and also that certain of these forms have power of inducing movement. The same is true of solid forms. The pyramid, the cube, the sphere, the ovoid and so on, are not only different in actual shape, but are different in sub-conscious value, and it is the subtle use of these forms which con-stitutes one of the chief virtues of sculpture. Architecture is the weaving of space into sensuous and significant pattern. Sculpture is allied with architecture in that it came into value to answer a demand for architectural ornament. Most great sculpture is thus subjected to the same pattern laws as the buildings it adorns. Nor does it matter whether the sculpture is put to other uses. The ornament on the handle of a knife, a clasp, or even a representative memorial of the dead, should be subject to certain laws which govern the general construction of the implement, the position for which the sculpture is intended. Thus, sculpture which is to be gripped in the hand must be in low relief, sculpture which is large and thus liable to accident should be exceedingly solid, sculpture in breakable material smaller or more compact than that in unbreakable.

Architecture is an art as abstract as music—it represents itself alone ; a house does not imitate a cave, nor a cathedral a grove of trees. It draws some of its appeal from the constructional stability and some from ornament. Sculpture derives its inspiration more directly from nature than does architecture and is thus less *abstract*. But in good sculpture we find the same emotional value derived from an interplay of space forms as in architecture ; and when the sculpture is used to decorate a building the forms of the sculpture must be in agreement with the general formulæ of the building itself. We find a definite relationship between the sculpture and the architecture of any great period. The solid sculpture of Egypt harmonizes with the massiveness of their temples, the delicacy of the Greek temple is reflected in their sculpture, and as Greek progresses from the strength and simplicity of the Doric to the complex and over-elaborated Corinthian, so the change can be noted in the sculpture ; force gives way to prettiness, significance to sensuality. The same can be noted in the Gothic or the Renaissance. To-day, architecture is a hopeless hotchpotch of all schools and all styles, we cannot even build sky-scrapers without clapping pseudo-Gothic ornament upon them, and most of the sculpture of to-day is in the same condition.

If we make a comparison between the foreleg of one of the lions in Trafalgar Square with the foreleg of a well-preserved sphinx we may perceive without much difficulty that the two differ. The leg of the former is at first sight more like a lion's leg than that of the latter. But the more we ponder over this lion's leg of bronze the less leonine it appears. We begin to perceive it as an ugly, almost shapeless mass of metal. Once we have recognized the superficial likeness nothing more is to be got from it. The Landseer lion is, therefore, an almost ideal decoration for a street through which people flash in buses or in cars. It is a one-look-and-no-more kind of decoration.

Let us turn our attention to the Sphinx. The leg is like enough to a leg to ensure recognition. It is, however, more of a description of the leg of a lion than an imitation—here are the claws, here the pads, here the joint, and so on. If we continue to gaze we find our eye gaining a subtle pleasure from the shape, the delicate curves ; we shall note how our eye tends to travel along the different planes of the surface ; and, finally, we should become conscious of a sense of order in the design of these planes and surfaces. We find, further, that there is nothing haphazard in the Sphinx. There is nothing that depends upon mere able realism for its emotional qualities; plane and curve meet and melt one into another, one shape is followed by another which emphasizes and is itself beautified by what has been perceived before.   We find within this semblance of lion body and human head a scheme of planned spaces as ordered as in a cathedral.   If the semblance is the melody, then the organization is the counterpoint, the resolution, the thorough bass.   The sense of the co-operation of Touch which all perceptions of space arouses (since the sense of space is a co-operation of the eyes and the grasping muscles and nerves) is vividly aroused by any good work of sculpture; we desire to pass our hands over the planes and curves, to caress with the fingers as if to complete the co-operation of the senses.

If now from the Sphinx we return to the lion in Trafalgar Square we recognize more clearly how clumsy an object it is.   What in nature is a coat of hair covering a structure of muscle, sinew and bone, here is not unlike a bronze sausage which has burst a little at the ends.   Save the pose, which is copied from that of the Sphinx, there is no *design* in the whole body, no spatial beauty, no rhythmic imagination.   It is the representation of a living animal in bronze, and as the life has gone the bronze is dead.   Nobody could imagine the bronze sausage of a foreleg lifted.   We touch now upon the problem of *life* in a work of art.

The most obvious aspect of life may be defined as the latent possibility for voluntary movement; even the most minute spores move in order to seize food, but almost all life which is patent to the senses perceptively possesses this power of movement.   Thus, a man in a cataleptic trance, though apparently dead, still stirs our imagination with the faint sensation of life.   But he stirs it thus only if we are *told* that he is cataleptic.   If we are ignorant of the fact of catalepsy, the man is to all appearances dead—and so in a similar way all living things when motionless appear to be without life: "Sleep the twin brother of Death."   Life is the *internal* property of living things.   The fable is well known of the critic who, mistaking a sleeping owl for a stuffed specimen, jeers at its lack of life.   He is confuted by the bird which, awakening, winks.   The poet is having a smack at a much-belaboured class, but in truth the critic was right, and the fable but illustrates a popular misconception of the problems of the artist. A sleeping bird can well appear dead and lifeless. It should have been the duty of a taxidermist to instil the animal (had it been stuffed) with a semblance of life. Real life is not an *external* property of living things ; but life must be an *external*, *visible* property of Art.

Life in sculpture is suggested by the design of the artist, and cannot be produced only by an accurate imitation of living forms. Motion is but relative ; the towering spire seems to swing against the moving clouds. And, as in drawing, suggestion of movement is conveyed by the fact that the eye is impelled to motion, so the motion-compelling quality of designed form and space (motion over plane and curve, interblending and contrast) conveys a suggestion to the mind that these forms though cast in bronze or carved in stone have movement possibilities. As we have shown, when the eye finally comes to rest, in an ellipse, for example, there remain possibilities of a sub-conscious sense of proportional relationship, so in the Sphinx in the field of vision remains the impression of these movement-inducing forms. This sense of the latent possibility of movement gives a sense of hidden life. Art thus creates the illusion of life ; and with justice Life may be called an internal property of living things, but an external property of art.

Of the drawing of a cube we have shown that the, as it were, distillation of the spatial properties which it achieves, and the illustration of these properties upon the flat, seems to make a comprehension of space more positive ; so this illusion of life produced in inanimate stone or metal seems to heighten the sensations of life and of living qualities. In a living thing life is a commonplace, though to see the tortoise move may excite admiration. But in a non-living thing the property of apparent life, the mystic sensation that this inanimate mass will move if we but turn the eyes away from it, is so remarkable that the meaning of life as life acquires an extraordinary value.

We have thus two powerful factors in sculpture which owe
their value to the æsthetic use of space ; the delight of the eye in
proportions of plane and of mass, and the illusion of life properties
which spatial proportions can induce. Both of these are due to
design. The pleasure which likeness to a known real object brings
must be recognized as a factor in art, but such a pleasure is less
vivid and less lasting, and suffers a speedy decay if we realize that
in an attempt to gain imitation the suggestion of life has been
sacrificed. The æsthetic factor of life is the work of the artist, it
depends upon his sense of design, upon what he draws from within
himself, and depends much less upon what he copies from nature.
We may say that nature is the bucket in which the water is drawn
from the well, but nature is not the water.

Space in painting has value similar to that in sculpture. The
Chinese artists ascribe to space (or infinity) the greatest value in
painting as an art ; and, because landscape gives to them the best
opportunity of space suggestion, they name landscape the most
profound of the plastic arts. In painting, space is produced by
three means : first, by imitation of the usual effects of nature ;
secondly, by the spatial properties of colour ; thirdly, by spatial
qualities of line, perspective, proportion, and so on. The eye can
delight in proportions of suggested space in painting even more than
it does in sculpture. In painting, space has a value more positive
than it has in actual life. The sense of space is distilled out—it
becomes a more concentrated draught.

Mr. Berenson, the founder of most modern criticism, in his
excellent work on the Florentine Painters calls this sense of space
in painting " tactile values," because the sense of space, as we have
explained, is allied with the muscles of touch. He says :

" How is it that an object the recognition of which in nature may
have given me no pleasure becomes when recognized in a picture
a source of æsthetic enjoyment ? The answer, I believe, depends
upon the fact that art stimulates to an unwonted activity psychical
processes which are in themselves the source of most (if not all) of our

pleasures and which here, free from disturbing physical sensations, never tend to pass over into pain. For instance, I am in the habit of realizing a given object with an intensity of two ; if I suddenly realize this familiar object with an intensity of four, I receive the immediate pleasure which accompanies a doubling of my mental activity. . . . This is what form does in painting ; it lends a higher co-efficient of reality to the object represented, with a consequent enjoyment of accelerated psychical processes and the exhilarating sense of increased capacity in the observer."

The drawing of a cube can give a heightened sense of the cubic, and in consequence " a sense of increased capacity in the observer " *as long as we concentrate upon this cubic quality*. But the drawing of a cube which we meet in ordinary life does not actually give either the sense of the cubic or a sense of increased capacity ; because in normal life we look at things not because we wish to see them precisely, but because we wish to make use of them. An examination paper on the details of most commonplace objects soon shows how many planes there are in our normal observation ; one is easily stumped with simple questions such as : draw the figures round the face of a clock, describe a lamp-post, etc. One of our habitual bad habits is that of substituting a formula for reality, we get a general idea of the face of a clock, or of a lamp-post, or of a cube, and that suffices us ; we travel round the world literally not perceiving one iota more than we are *forced* to see in order to survive. When interest is aroused by something of an unusual nature, we do look and for a while we must concentrate.*

The mere fact that the cube can arouse this sense of " tactile values," or space sensations, gives to it an æsthetic content, but the fact that the cube is a common formula more than destroys this

* This explains the rapid loss of pleasure which so many purchasers experience in a work of second-rate order. The compelling interest of the picture is quickly exhausted, and we begin to regard it without concentration. With a masterpiece the interest deepens by long examination. But even a masterpiece can be exhausted by time, and become boring by too intimate an acquaintanceship. It then needs a rest, during which its virtues will revive. The virtues of a merely pleasing picture do not revive thus.

æsthetic value because it does not attract our interest.   Our imagination is not sufficiently aroused, we are not stimulated to look at the
cube a moment longer than is necessary for recognition.   Thus the
sense of space is only valuable æsthetically when it is allied to
something which claims attention, and which seduces the mind to
concentration.   This is provided by the design of the artist, the
physiological values of rhythmic order, or of harmonious colour, the
interweaving of surfaces, and so on, which create a sensation of life.

I

CHAPTER XII

THE VALUE OF ART

THE value of art to us depends upon what value we place upon life, and before we can really settle the question we must to some extent grapple with the problem of existence. Life, as we see it, is divided into three sections: work, leisure, and sleep. There is a general tendency to preach that work is noble, leisure useless and on the whole degrading. The practice of the world contradicts this statement. There is a unanimous tendency to struggle towards a position in which labour becomes no longer a necessity. The leisured are envied by their fellow-men. What is work for? It is to keep the world going on; it is the hard necessity of our existence; and only because it is so potently necessary do we elevate it to a virtue in order to take the edge from its undesirability. Play and leisure, since they are so tempting, have to be degraded to vices in order to preserve a balance. Work is useful to keep the world going on. Gorky makes one of his characters say, " We work to eat and we eat to work." Obviously work as work cannot be an ideal. The clamour for labour-saving devices, the premium put upon invention shows how, in spite of our creed of the nobility of work, we endeavour to lessen the burden of such a horrible nobility. No, work as work is an evil of existence. If the ideal that work alone is noble were correct, the value of life diminishes to a negligible quantity.

If life is to have any real value to humanity, it is because life itself and the recognition of life have a real value. There is then a virtue in the increase of the recognition of life's value. Slavery is a degrading condition, and all work done merely to avoid starvation or chaos is slavery to the domination of earth and to the necessity of existence. The demand of every new experiment in civilization is primarily a demand for more liberty from the earth. In reality leisure is the desirable thing of life, and in spite of the fears of the moralists it is rightly so to be considered.

If man were habitually of a lazy nature, then leisure would be, no doubt, the evil which it is depicted. But very few men, save in enervating climates, can survive the infinite boredom which continued inaction brings. The man whom fortunate circumstances relieves from the slavery of compulsory work fills it with some activity. It is curious that this activity usually takes the form of some kind of pursuit of which the aim is the enhancement of the consciousness of life or the development of faculties which indirectly lead to life enhancement. The sportsman is engaged in the refinement of certain faculties the exercise of which brings to him an increased sense of the value of existence. The advance in civilization, which marks us from the primitive savage, is the result not of labour but of leisure, that is, of the spontaneous activities of man freed from the demands of mere existence. The first great civilization of which we have definite record arose from such a cause in Egypt or Mesopotamia where, owing to the peculiarities of the rivers, the general population enjoyed each year between the harvests long periods of leisure during which the people improved and adorned their existence.

Humanity has two means by which it can appreciate the value of existence: the Bodily and the Mental. These two cannot properly be separated, for the body (or physical part) cannot be appreciated without the co-operation of the mental (or spiritual) faculties, while the mind is under the dominance of the body and its well-being. Yet there is a differentiation. Thus, the bodily pleasures are intimately associated with the actual facts of living. Mere physical prowess does not excite a large amount of general interest or praise. The sports which awaken the most intense enthusiasm are those which involve a combination of physical perfection with mental subtlety, and if we could imagine a world in which all physical perfection were equal, we should find that the interest of a sport would be solely concentrated upon the mental subtlety displayed by the players. There would be no fun in watching a foot race if we were assured that all the competitors would tie at the post, but there would still remain much enjoyment in watching the combination and mental work displayed in a game of football. To a large extent, the value of sport as an enhancement of the sense of life depends also upon the physical condition of the sportsman. The man who cannot run cannot enjoy playing a game of football, nor the one with rheumatism a contest at golf. He may derive a certain pleasure from the watching of the game, but he does not get a physical pleasure from this. The only pleasures which are open to *universal* enjoyment are mental pleasures, that is to say, pleasures in which the actual demands of existence are no longer active. The contemplative pleasures are the highest resources of mankind, those farthest removed from the animal.

The pleasures of the body increase the joy of life by stimulating the physical life itself, but we remain tied to the consciousness of our bodies. On the other hand, the æsthetic (or contemplative) pleasures bring with them a sense of dissociation from the body. In the physical pleasure the mind can watch the action of the rest of the body, that is to say, the pleasure is within our body and we remain aware of the body. But when the pleasure is seated in the mind itself the pleasure is more difficult to localize. Hence we derive a feeling of release from bodily bonds, which is inspiring. In the case of " Space " or of " Life " in art, as we have explained, the sensation seems to become more vivid because it is separated from ordinary surroundings (as the drawing of a cube seems more positively cubic than the cube itself, or the life of a statue more living than real life), so in the mind the release from the consciousness of physical life lends to life itself a more intense meaning and therefore a greater vitality.

The function of all good art and, indeed, of all forms of real beauty, is to increase the sense of the value of life.

But we may yet be unable to trace the connection between the value of art and the means by which this value is reached. We have said that art is the creation of beauty, and that beauty is life-communicating or has " vitality." But how does this depend upon these things of which we have spoken ; how do the fusion of colour, space and form into pictorial composition become life-communicating, and what are the relative values of each in producing the desired result ?

The answer to the question lies, I feel, in the normal tendency of humanity to judge by comparative standards. If we were suddenly transported to the moon, we should not realize that the force of gravity had enormously diminished, but that we had become both unusually strong and unusually light. The strength would increase our sense of vitality, but the decrease in weight would do the reverse. However, we should probably not feel that it was we who were unaltered and the conditions different, although this fact might be well known to us. We should instinctively imagine the conditions to be the same ; that the alteration had taken place in ourselves. If we were to seize a rock which would weigh upon earth a hundredweight, and hurl it from us, we should have almost as much pride in the feat as though the rock really were a hundred-weight heavy. A phenomenon of a similar kind takes place in the arts. Our perceptions are, as it were, suddenly relieved from an oppressing sense of a kind of gravity—the looking at articles in order to use them. We do not mean that the world is always appreciated with the intention of definitely making use of it, but no matter what the object regarded it is considered at first from this point of view.

Colour, space, and form make up the visible world through which it is of the utmost importance that we should be able to find our way. Touch is allied with the perception of space. But these properties of sight are important principally because they are useful, and this very utility prevents us from understanding them as things

to be enjoyed through the senses. Thus we find that the first feeling
of beauty (or enjoyment of the senses) is perceived in that quality
which is the least ordinarily useful, the quality of colour.   The
barbarian loves colour, and even to the Greeks colour was so valuable
a constituent of beauty that their statuary was painted.   The quality
of form is perceived next as an æsthetic value and, last of all, the
fundamentally important value of space.

In the arts, these perceptions by which we make our way through
the world are suddenly relieved from the mere demands of existence
itself.   In ordinary life the demands of existence weigh down upon
our perceptive powers in the same way that the power of gravity
limits us in the use of our strength.   On the moon we should
suddenly get the sensation of extraordinary internal force ; in the
arts we receive a sense that the powers of perception are doubled
or quadrupled in penetration.   This reaction produces the feeling
of more power to overcome existence ; a sense of superior life is
communicated to us.

But since each quality of perception has a different value in life,
so each quality in the arts appears to have a somewhat different
power of life-communication. Colour as colour is not supremely
valuable in life, in fact, colour as colour is of so unstable a nature, as
we have shown, that it may be said to have little independent
existence.   Therefore the pleasure to be derived from colour alone
is not intensely " vital."   We derive an exquisite and sensuous joy
from colour, it is true ; but this enjoyment stops short of the highest.
However exquisite a series of daubs of colour might be in colour
relationship, if they were comparatively formless the attention
would not long be held by them, and our eyes would be drawn to
other things.   The sensation of pleasure aroused would be almost
immediate, but it might not last.   Yet the importance of colour
must not be overlooked.   Though in life colour is not intensely
necessary, yet the colours have quite definite physiological reactions
—the excitement of red, the calmness of blue, etc.—by means of
which a mood can be evoked, and by means of which the other

æsthetic values may be enhanced. Form and movement are the two visual functions of life which are most positively useful. These are, in consequence, the most commonly potent of the life-communicating qualities. In a non-representative (or abstract) art the problem of form reduces itself to a fusion of fine shapes with the suggestions of movement. As soon as realism is allowed, as in sculpture or pictorial art, two other factors come into play in the imitative quality of form and what we may call the *æsthetic paraphrase*.

An imitation alone does not always give beauty of shape, nor does it suggest movement. Instantaneous photographs of any kind of moving object show that movement is not given by imitative form. Therefore, in order to produce the real beauty of shape and creation of movement, often a considerable compromise had to be undertaken. The mere recognition of a " likeness " to nature need not produce an effect upon the senses, because the recognition is not itself the direct work of the senses. Recognition in this case would be the work of memory. The sentiment of beauty, however, is primarily the work of the senses. The difference between the emotional value of the circle and of the ellipse are not because we have memories or ideas about the circle or the ellipse, but because these figures are direct stimulants upon the senses. Thus, in the compromise which is undertaken between imitative form and harmonious form, that quality which possesses the least absolute value, the imitative, is the first which is (or may be) discarded. The frankness with which this has been recognized by the present-day artists is the chief factor which so dismays the public. In the ancient times when the formal qualities of an art were classic, that is, when they were more or less circumscribed by a convention, there is little doubt that the concentration of the public upon one or two problems only of beauty of form must have educated the public eye to a high appreciation of beauty within those circumscribed limits, but would have atrophied appreciation beyond the same limits. Thus, the Egyptian would be able properly to appreciate the beauty of form in Egyptian works, and also the Gothic his own, but the Egyptian would not have appreciated the Gothic, nor vice versa.

To-day the public only consciously appreciates form as imitation. Even when the form is a clearly organized and vital composition, the public still imagines that the imitation moves it to pleasure. Sometimes, when there is frankly a divergence from imitation as in primitive art or conventional art, the public excuses itself on the ground that there is beauty and that the artist was *doing his best*. The consequence is that when a work is presented in which the imitative quality is not too much insisted upon, nor which falls into one of the categories of ancient (and therefore learned) deviations from imitation, the public becomes confused and exasperated.

Passing from shape and movement we come to the third perception of use to life, that of space, which is the last developed, as well as the last to be consciously used in painting. The baby sees colour and shape long before it is able to appreciate distance, for the perceptions of colour and of shape are optical perceptions only, while the space perception demands an interaction of sight and touch. In Western painting, the spatial value has been appreciated and used by a few artists of genius. Actually, it is the most important of the visual qualities in the function of life for the spectator. Without the spatial sense, existence would be impossible. The blind man survives without a sense either of colour or of visual form, but his sense of spatial relationships must be extremely sensitive to compensate for the loss of the other qualities. Owing to its importance, the spatial quality when dissociated from the needs of life has a most vivid life-communicating value for the spectator. The sensation of organized space produces in the observer the effect of *Infinity* in art.

CHAPTER XIII

DERAIN AND VLAMINCK

WE have kept in the background, somewhat deliberately, the personalities which have been involved in the struggle which the initiators of the modern movements had to undertake in order to propagate their particular visions of Art. We have kept to a study of artistic processes themselves rather than to a study of the characters of the artists involved in the elucidation of those processes.

We have said of the Impressionists that they turned from a study of the appearance of an object to a study of the means by which that appearance was perceived; but we have not tried to indicate the enormous mental courage and force of personal initiative which lie behind that step. No higher human courage can be imagined than that of the man who affirms a new aspect of truth, or who questions something hitherto believed to be truth by public opinion. The precursors and initiators of the modern artistic vision were in the position of a few men who defied the whole world; and not only the world as a physical or practical fact, but the world as telepathic, psychological fact, a world far more oppressive than the former.

We must not forget to take into consideration the whole subconscious attitude of the public towards art, in order to estimate what in fact was the quality residing in men like Monet, Pissarro, Cézanne, Seurat, Signac, Van Gogh, etc. An artist does not wish to be misunderstood; for if he is not understood his whole artistic life is a failure. Nor, in spite of popular belief, does the artist really delight in shocking the public. The true end and aim of the artist's effort is *appreciation;* he is pathetically eager to be loved.

121

But he wishes to be loved at a proper level, at his own level. He is like a woman who is bold enough to persist that her husband shall like her for herself; and not because she becomes merely a sort of human cushion upon which the man can leave his own imprint.

It is clear that in order to face the tremendous weight of public opprobrium, an innovating artist must be pressed forward by an equally great weight of inner conviction. His art becomes a faith, for which he is a martyr, though often an unwilling one. Or, he is a Columbus who may be likely from time to time to entertain doubts whether there is really land on the other side of the apparently boundless ocean. But once the land has been discovered the Corteses, the Olids, the Pizarros come after, not differing much, perhaps, in sheer elevation of personal courage, yet differing considerably in the fine quality of that courage. The *first* discoverer who works by a sort of divine intuition is a man of different fibre from those men who set forth when discovery had become the fashion.

We have already considered certain aspects of this question in the chapter upon Matisse, but we may now review it again from a different point of view. In reference to Matisse we developed the suggestion that there are two main different varieties of painters, those who have something to say, and those who know how to say it. We have pointed out that these are not—as human nature never is—separated clearly, but are blended with and merge into one another.

When we examine the work of the first Post-Impressionist painters we find that each develops, by slow degrees and by natural researches, into a technique which expresses the particular truths he is trying to convey. Once the artist has found the method of transcribing his convictions he is satisfied. From thence onwards his technique expands slowly, and only because he discovers in practice a further extension of his artistic convictions. Thus we find that Signac, Gauguin, and Rousseau do not develop their techniques much beyond a quite early presentation, because their artistic ideas remain almost stable. Cézanne, on the other hand, goes on developing until the last; but it is a slow logical development. The later water-colours which are almost without local colour—in which the colouring represents space sensation and emphasis of solidity and of construction—are developments almost prophesied by the beginnings of his individual vision.

The technique of these painters and the novelties which grew out of the techniques seem always to be consecutive developments: they appear natural and inevitable to us, now that we can at leisure study the whole career of the artist. Thus Van Gogh accepted Pointillism as a reasonable method of painting light. The peculiarity of Van Gogh *grows* out of the dynamic fury which would not allow him to accumulate small spots of colour until the canvas was covered. The method was too slow for the rapidity of the artist's imagination. In consequence his spots spread to ribbons and slashes of interblended paint.

When we come to the works of the second period of modern artists we note a difference of attitude from those of the early Post-Impressionists. This second period was called in Paris artistic slang " Les Fauves," and by this title we can continue to call it for convenience. The " Wild Beasts " of art, who included such painters as Matisse, Derain, Vlaminck, Dufy, Friesz, Chagall, and most of the modern realists, were characterized at one period by a sort of restlessness akin to that of a carnivorous animal tracking its prey. We may, perhaps, emphasize the difference between the two generations of artists by an image.

We can liken the earlier group to a scientist who is analysing a mineral in which he suspects the presence of an elusive and rare chemical. He extracts and refines, extracts and refines once more, until the pure substance sought for remains. The second group seems more like an experimenter who is trying to invent (or synthesize) a substance, the properties of which he has in his mind, but of the exact manufacture of which he is uncertain. He will try combination after combination of likely substances until the compound proves its presence by the appearance of its preconceived properties. These two processes are very different, although they may be aimed at producing the same substance. Something of an analagous nature has taken place in art. Although we can find in Cézanne or Van Gogh evidences of frank borrowing from other artists, Cézanne especially having borrowed from El Greco, from Poussin, and from many of the Old Masters, Van Gogh having copied and transposed Millet, we do not find amongst these painters the persistent examination and practical exploitation of the past in the way which has been carried out by the younger men. It is a common reproach levelled at the modern artists that they despise the Old Masters, that they do not understand what realistic drawing is. In truth, Picasso and Derain, the leaders of two schools of modern thought in art matters, have always been the most persistent students of the past and probably know far more about the Louvre than most of their academic opponents.

The series of painters between Cézanne and Rousseau represents a burst of genius paralleled only by that of the Renaissance. Indeed, the times are somewhat similar : in each case we have a new century growing out of an old one. The chief difference which separates these painters from the Fauves, who in reality *organized* the modern movement, lies in the change of attitude towards art which we have just noted.

I think we may say that the painters of the first epoch did not recognize clearly what they had been doing. Although Cézanne said, " I am the primitive of a school which will grow up after me," he could not quite realize how little he was primitive. Nor, if he were in truth the primitive of the modern effort, could he foresee what would be the nature of his followers. He could not have anticipated the amazing variety, vitality—and, indeed, impertinence—of some of his disciples. If Cézanne in 1869 could have seen 1920 in a magic glass, and if he could have realized that the Independents of to-day claim him as their leader, chief inspiration and fountain-head, he would probably have committed suicide forthwith. I should like to see Cézanne's ghost reading what

ANDRÉ DERAIN

LANDSCAPE

André Lhote has said about him and Picasso in *La Nouvelle Revue française*.

But the Fauves realized quite clearly what had been done. The intoxication of self-consciousness began to haunt them. For an artist it may be dangerous to know too much; pedantry is a vice which fixes too easily into the human system. It is, perhaps, easier for an artist to find his way through the dangers of the unknown than through those of the known. There were three ways of seeking salvation for these men. The one way Matisse tried. He thought himself back to five years old; having purged his vision from conventional preconceptions, he then tried to see the subject in directly visual relationships of line and colour. Another way was to learn more, to know everything: to get the whole scale of artistic effort arranged in proper proportion, and from this standpoint to push forward to creation. This road was followed by Derain and Picasso. A third way was to get a new impulse from some strange though vital art which had conserved enough simplicity to be capable of development: this way was used by Vlaminck and, as we have shown, by Modigliani.

During the course of these attempts to find the peculiar compound in which the æsthetic vitality could be presented we find that Matisse before achieving an artificial innocence experimented with the French academism of the Artistes Français, with Bonnard, Seurat and Signac, with Gauguin, and he has trifled with some of the manifestations of Picasso, as well as with Marquet. Picasso begins with Steinlen and has passed through phases of Puvis de Chavannes, Daumier, Cézanne (in conjunction with Derain), El Greco, Negro art, Braque (at the beginnings of Cubism), and finally Ingres. Derain has tested the properties of Courbet, Marquet, Toulouse Lautrec, Gauguin, Cézanne, the Negro sculpture, Byzantine and primitive Italian—Vlaminck developed directly out of Cézannism under the impulse (but not the imitation) of Negro art.

Derain is surely one of the most learned of the painters of to-day —he has been, if anything, oppressed by too much knowledge. He

was present at the initiation of Cubism and made a few experiments
in that direction, but he declined to follow the exciting lead of
Picasso.   During the last eight years he must have often wondered
if he has been right.   Derain was, perhaps, not fanciful enough to
be seduced by Cubism.   His art is truly French, a rational development of the classical tradition, modified by the impress of Cézanne,
and modified again, naturally, by the personal impress of Derain
himself.

Derain

We may roughly define a classical art as one which is contained
within certain boundaries, an art which is definite within frontiers.
It has become a custom to call only that art which is derived by
tradition from Greece classical art; but I think that it is possible
to extend the boundaries of the word.   Every art which is represented by a model formula is classical.   Egyptian art, Chinese art,
Byzantine art, and so on; each has a different classicism of its own.
And we see Derain, in searching to re-establish the boundaries of
his own classicism, testing in turn the classicism of the manifestations of art of other days.   A rather ridiculous image of the difference
between Derain and Vlaminck springs into my mind.   I see them,
Derain as a cat and Vlaminck as a dog, set down in a house, the
problem being to reach the open air.   Vlaminck hurries through
one or two rooms, and finding a window open dashes out—into a
walled garden.   Derain, as a cat, goes carefully through every room,
peeps through every window, is not satisfied with the prospect,
explores farther, and finally emerges on to the roof, amongst the
chimney-pots, tiles and bits of broken brick and plaster.

I think that of the whole Fauve group, Derain is, perhaps, the
artist who has innately the largest proportion of subtlety of mind.
But he is a subtle mind with too vivid a conscience.   It was Derain
who first grasped the real value of Cézanne.   Derain was probably
the first who produced studies showing that the novel structure of
Cézanne's compositions had been *understood* by a painter, and who
thus revealed a new path along which pointed the finger of the old
man of Aix.   Up to that time the chief impulse had been derived

ANDRÉ DERAIN
PORTRAIT OF THE PAINTER KISLING

from Van Gogh and from Gauguin, especially from the latter. Thus the line to Cubism passes through Derain.

In general the art of Derain denies picturesque interest even more rigidly than did Cézanne. My simile of the roof tops with chimney-pots and bits of broken plaster is justified. Derain shapes the grandiose out of the despicable. He further denies himself even the luxury—or the sensuality—of colour. The influence of the later Impressionists, of the Pointillists and of Gauguin had created a school of painting in which *effects* of colour are pushed almost to the limits. Colour, as I have explained earlier, can lose its power to please. The mistaken efforts of some of the Independents, and more powerfully yet, the sickly, almost nauseating deluge of colour which poured from the Salon des Beaux Arts, made serious artists reflect upon the qualities of colour itself. One does not reach to fine colour by piling tint against tint, by flinging vermilion or cerise against viridian.

Derain restricted his palette more and more until his colour conception has become as severe as his ideas of the picturesque. This does not mean that Derain has not shown powers as a colourist. He has followed and amplified the colour experiments of Gauguin. He has clearly proved that if he wished to use pure colour he can do so. His palette of few tints, of a few degraded greens, of ochres and siennas, of earthy reds, of iron greys, is formed by deliberate choice and not by necessity. Derain represents the natural reaction of the man of instinctive good taste against excess. There is a strange delight in his contrasts of iron grey, green, and sienna. This restrained colour often gives a sensation akin to that produced by the presence of a simple, honest man at some frivolous *reunion*.

Derain's best work is full of those qualities which we have already discussed, and which excite the sub-conscious appreciations of vitality; and he resolutely puts on one side any delectability which may detract from or disturb the clear perception of his aims. One can almost, as it were, read his compositions, his colour schemes are as distinctly stated as print.

We may contrast with Derain the other painter, Vlaminck, who was at one time closely associated with him. At one time Derain and Vlaminck formed a little group by themselves, *l'école du Chatou*. Perhaps in studying the landscape of early summer in Chatou one may find the sources of Derain's present colour schemes. But the *école du Chatou* was a transitory affair. Save for an equal enthusiasm there is little in common between Vlaminck and Derain. Vlaminck, although not a Cubist, is also one of the artists responsible for Cubism. His painting is so personal that it can have little weight in the future development of painting, but his discoveries and his practice in art have already left a profound impression upon the art of to-day. At the moment when Vlaminck brought to notice the art of the Congo, techniques were becoming complicated. There was in some sort a struggle between the Pointillism of Signac and the divided tones of Cézanne. Negro art proved that with extreme simplicity the highest emotional pitch can be reached. It showed that extraordinary blend of rich rounded surfaces contrasted with rigid angular outlines, out of which the finest abstract pattern may be created.

Vlaminck had been studying the cubic composition of Cézanne and, along the lines which Cézanne had set down, had been developing a spatial composition of his own, carefully constructed, and somewhat rigid in presentation. Without throwing away what he had gained from Cézannism, Vlaminck proceeded to simplify and to intensify his pictures. He is the most passionate painter of to-day. There is a sort of fury driving his brush, a fury of making something. Though in technique he is very different, he is a sort of sombre Van Gogh.

Every artist works from that part of his personality which is most creative ; and it is impossible to say that one part is better than the other. We can only judge between results. A picture can be the result of long meditation like Derain's " Le Samedi " which took five years to complete : or it may be the hurried grasping after a sensation which must be seized and recorded before it can change its quality, such as these pictures of Van Gogh or of Vlaminck. A

MAURICE DE VLAMINCK
EARLY SNOW

picture of Vlaminck's is not a " moment of emotion recorded in tranquillity," but a " moment of emotion recorded within its duration." His pictures are records of states of being. Shorthand methods of putting the spectator into direct contact with the painter's experience. Naturally, as the emotions of Vlaminck vary, his pictures are variable in intensity. One cannot always be at fever-heat and remain sane.

In a way, Vlaminck's painting makes one think of a musician tearing improvisations out of the bowels of a double bass. This sombre construction of black umber and viridian, relieved by dashes of crude vermilion, Prussian blue and white ; this harshly cubic vision of small houses contrasted with indeterminate masses of trees ; and earth which merges into sky.

Vlaminck's painting and his vision is so positive that one has to be positive about it. It is a painting to which one cannot be indifferent. Like the man, it has either friends or enemies. The chief fault with us to-day is that we are apt to be indeterminate. Modern social conditions do not encourage the growth of positive personalities. They are too uncomfortable for our commercial state. Men of the Vlaminck nature are positive dangers to the creed of submission which we must learn in order to live comfortably with the machine and the factory owner.

Vlaminck, like Van Gogh, is a spiritual revolutionary.

We may again formulate the difference between Derain and Vlaminck by saying that Derain seems to work for the result, while with Vlaminck the impulse lies in the very work itself. In this latter quality Vlaminck again resembles Van Gogh. The Dutch painter drew on everything he could reach, café tables, bits of newspaper, and his friends were forced to protect their furniture by covering it with a paper suitable for drawing upon. In Derain we find that his schemes and compositions have a deliberate quality ; even when they are unexpected, one feels that the unexpected has been prepared for us ; Vlaminck's unexpectedness is almost always spontaneous.

K

There seems to be one drawback to Vlaminck's method of working. Galton in his first experiments in the sub-conscious mind (since developed by Freud) discovered that one possesses unconsciously a limited stock of instinctive ideas, and that unless we exercise considerable selection the same thought repeats itself even under different stimuli. One would expect to find the same phenomenon recurring with a painter who relies chiefly on impulse and feeling. One's expectation is justified. We find in Vlaminck a certain repetition which tends to become monotony if one sees too many of his pictures at a time ; the same is true of Modigliani. But perhaps this is not a serious defect. A picture is not a book. One does not have the whole of a painter's production on the wall, but one or two chosen examples. Thus when the pictures of Vlaminck are spread about the world by the natural processes, this question of monotony disappears. One does not blame an author because his work is published in an edition of several thousands. The Old Masters repeated themselves and copied one another over and over again.

Derain has been called by André Salmon the balance wheel (or engine governor) of the modern movements, and the image has a large amount of justice if one considers the steady development of his art, which pursues its way little affected by the hectic years which tortured the Salon des Indépendants before the war. Curiously enough, he is one of the modern artists the least known in England. Yet he is probably the one who most approaches the cautious acceptance of novel ideas which is one of our characteristics. He has also in his work a touch of that cultivated archaism which is natural to our Gothic blood. Out of this fusion of Cézanne, Gauguin, and the primitive European painters, Derain has made a personal art which is now leaning back to touch the French academism of Ingres and Courbet. It is, I think, possible that Derain, like Picasso, knows his art galleries too well. The great arts of the past arose to their peculiar excellencies because they despised the arts of their own past. Thus a Renaissance architect, contemptuous of the Gothic, would restore a Gothic church with Renaissance additions. There is in this attitude a certain truth to one's culture and social conditions which is very healthy, and I feel that these harkings back to the past, on the part of artists like Derain and Picasso, would be the equivalent of a harking back by Renaissance to Gothic.

Although Futurism was a literary, patriotic, and sentimental Italian creed which added nothing to art, it was right in its insistence that we depend too much upon picture galleries. The great arts of the past arose because the artists were true to their own civilizations, and only admitted the *unconscious* influence of the past. It is necessary for the artists of to-day to be true to their civilization also. Cézanne stands, like Giotto, at the junction, with a foot in each culture; but Derain comes, let us say, in the position of Uccello, who would have ruined his work had he turned back to the Byzantine. Derain's last figure-painting comes back almost definitely to French classicism, although beneath the presentation one can perceive the structure which he has drawn from Negro art; his latest landscape might be the work of a different artist, he returns so much to Poussin in order to escape the accusation of Cézannism that he is in danger of getting from Scylla into Charybdis. I feel that to-day Derain is most characteristic in his still lives.

CHAPTER XIV

CUBISM

RUSKIN, although he states distinctly that in order to present one truth properly, an artist may show everything else untruthfully, would have tried to limit the artist to a statement of a certain order of nature truths only : to a sort of crude materialism which he calls " worshipping the *works* of the Creator." But, indeed, we cannot limit the boundaries of art until we are sure of the boundaries of the human mind. Every race has its art, which not only may be externally different from, but may be contradictory to the art of another land. At a certain level of acceptance if the Greeks are right the Egyptians are wrong ; practically every external ideal of Greece is contradicted by Egypt. To appreciate both arts at their proper value we must dive a little deeper into the human consciousness.

We can make a sort of mental image of these diverse sorts of beauty if we compare them to the action of gravity, and the act of standing upright on the world. We probably have an idea that the two ends of a long building are parallel, since each end is upright. But precisely for this reason they are not parallel. No two lines which are perpendicular to the earth can be parallel, because each is the projection of a *radius* of the earth, and thus the two sides of, say, Buckingham Palace if projected as far as Sirius would have spread as widely apart as the width of the Milky Way.

In a similar way we may imagine different forms of beauty as having uprightness with regard to a sort of centre of gravity of beauty, yet without any necessity of being parallel. Now if one insists only upon *parallelism*, one has the right to say that the man in

ANDRÉ LHOTE
PORTRAIT OF MME LHOTE

Australia is standing on his head ; and with a similar point of view from the art of Greece, that of Egypt is also standing on its head. But in this question parallelism does not come into play, one does not stand upright with regard to an imaginary straight line, but with regard to a centre of radiation. Thus, when Ruskin says that an artist may deny other truths in order to state one truth clearly, he is thinking in a *parallelism* : When one is stating one *upright* truth the other truths are not parallel (and therefore cannot be included as true) from that particular standpoint.

We stand upright upon this world by an instinct, and as we move about this world we change our direction in space so that we remain upright. But there is one object which is capable of moving about the globe without changing its direction in space—or parallelism. This is the gyroscope. The tendency of the gyroscope is always to remain pointing in the same direction. If a man walks from the North Pole to the equator, his head will begin by pointing at the pole star and end by pointing at Orion, but the gyroscope will begin by pointing at the pole star and at the equator will still be pointing at the pole star.

In our appreciation of art we seem to possess this gyroscopic tendency. To the gyroscope naturally the man in the Antipodes is standing on his head ; and to us as long as we ignore the centre of gravity of art we shall be unable to appreciate more than one aspect of the artistic manifestations. The direction of the gyroscope can only be altered by force, the gyroscope resists change. So, too, we resist change in our æsthetic appreciations. The person who says, " I know nothing about art ; but I know what I like," is merely boasting of his mechanical, brainless, gyroscopic immobility. We cannot know what we like, or rather we cannot know what we are capable of liking, until we have moved our gyroscopic head through several degrees at least. Cubism is worthy of a concentrated study because it is most capable of reducing the spin of our gyroscope, and will therefore put us more into contact with a sense of true universal uprightness of beauty. If we can appreciate architecture we can

appreciate Cubism, for Cubism is the painter's equivalent to architecture.   Or we may say architecture is a variety of Cubist sculpture.

Cubism developed into the art of organized space, linear form,
movement, and colour, dissociated from realistic appearance.   It
represents, if you will allow it, the plain roast meat of art, basted with
a little philosophic and mathematical gravy.

In architecture and applied art which are non-representative
we allow the art to be governed by its own rules.   We admit the
loveliness of the Chinese vase, or of the cathedral, or of a Persian
carpet, but as soon as the work takes on a certain veneer of likeness
to nature (or representation) we attempt to dismiss the criteria by
which we formerly judged, in order to set up a new set of laws which
we demand to be first fulfilled before we will give our senses play.
These are the dogmas of realism.   We say with conviction, this vase
is more beautiful than that one—or this cathedral, or this rug as
the case may be.   We judge by instinct, and can give no chapter
or verse of reason other than this instinctive judgment.   We realize
that equal values in beauty arouse similar sensations of pleasure ;
and, though we cannot compare the actual beauties of vase or
cathedral, we can compare the different qualities of pleasure, and in
comparing note that they are of the same order, are stimulated
through the same means, and rely upon the same instinctive
judgment.

Applied art merges by imperceptible degrees into pictorial art.
There is no point at which we can stop our judgment by instinct in
order to substitute our judgment by " canons of realism."   Essentially the applied art and the pictorial art are the same in basis.

So that we can say : " When a painting is perfect, its æsthetic
value is no higher than that of a vase or of a cathedral, it produces
upon us the same effect, by the same means."

Realism does add nothing to the æsthetic value of a work of art.

Cubism is *au fond* a method of relieving pictorial art from the
weight of realism or of representation of any kind.   It would
isolate those qualities which one judges instinctively in the vase or

the cathedral ; and thus would force the spectator to judge once more instinctively. It refuses any place to knowledge in æsthetic appreciation. As we have shown in Chapter XI., the qualities of a cube are more poignantly to be appreciated when we must concentrate exclusively upon these qualities ; so the three fundamental qualities of art would have an enhanced effect if one were able to taste them in purity.

This requires a deliberate change of attitude on the part of the spectator. It demands a concentration upon shape as shape ; space suggestion as space suggestion, colour for colour virtues alone. Cubism creates an art, unrealistic in itself, but founded upon the contemplation of nature. It began as an attempt to produce a fusion between certain æsthetic ideas which were discovered about the same time and which have been pursued separately by different artists.

(1) The composition of space suggestion, originated by Cézanne, developed by Derain, Friesz, Vlaminck.

(2) The emotional quality of simplified form, discovered in Negro art by Vlaminck, carried on by him, by Derain, Modigliani, etc.

(3) The pure colour, developing through Van Gogh, Gauguin, Signac, etc., carried on by Matisse and Dufy.

The appreciation of painting as a sort of music, that is, of something which is beautiful in itself, beautiful because of harmonies, because of linear movements and suggestions of space, involves some change in the sense of reality itself. Vision becomes no longer material and actual like that of the camera, but all-embracing like the ether. One must become possessed of a sense of universal vision. Galton, whom we have quoted before, says :

" I find that a few persons can, by what they describe as a kind of touch-sight, visualize at the same moment all round a solid body. Many can do so nearly, but not altogether round that of a terrestrial globe. An eminent mineralogist assures me that he is able to imagine simultaneously all the sides of a crystal with which he is familiar.   I may be allowed to quote a curious faculty of my own in respect to this.   It is exercised only occasionally and in dreams, or rather in nightmares, but under those circumstances I am perfectly conscious of embracing an entire sphere in a single perception.   It appears to lie within my mental eyeball and to be viewed centripetally."

I have noticed personally that this faculty of viewing all round a solid body, this touch-sight, increases its powers very considerably with practice.   The concentration upon space as an artistic value further enlarges the powers of touch-sight, and probably most good artists possess this quality in a fair state of development.

The spatial conception of a street will ignore all accidentals, it will concentrate upon the size and weight of the houses, the box-like sensations of structure, sensations of stability.   It is no longer a question of optics, but a combination of vision and of comprehension. This sensation as that of space itself lies beyond pure vision.   The house is understood not as one face only but as a whole ; so that as one submits to the space sensation one admits not only the particular view at which one is gazing, but every possible view of the several objects which compose a scene.   This idea of nature tends more and more away the impermanencies of direct vision, to rest upon the permancies of consciousness.

Painting inspired by such sensations tends to become the painter's version of a literary description : it is " the pig and the wolf struggled in his face " put into a plastic form.   Thus, an artist such as Braque will brood over a still-life arrangement, and will later on reconstruct an image of that which formed in the strange recesses of his mind during this contemplation. We find here an explanation of the constant recurrence of printed words which appear in Cubist pictures.   Words, and particularly printed words, are symbols which are more vivid as *memoria* than any other visual objects.   They have forms of letters which are so conventionalized that they are constant, and they have a meaning which is detached from the form.   Thus the cup

Collection of M. Fuss-Amore

OTHON FRIEZ. (1909)
THE BATHERS

as fact has a million forms and only one meaning—that is itself —but the word CUP has a constant form, and a double meaning— that of itself as a collection of letters and that of its significance as cup. We see, then, that the constant intrusion of words into Cubist pictures has a logical psychological value. Picasso, as a Spaniard, has also national emotions concerning the guitar, which he introduces with perfect reason. Unfortunately, the disciples have not the inventiveness of the leaders, and guitars are thrust into Cubist compositions without rhyme or reason until one is as nauseated with the instrument as Wyndham Lewis is with the illegitimate descendants of Cézanne's apples.

Cubism developed roughly thus :

(1) Reduction of a picture to the chief elements of space suggestion.

(2) Combination of two properties of modern art; of the space painting of Cézannism, with simplified emotional form (or Negroism) in low-relief.

(3) Transference of this low-relief combination to a flat surface.

(4) Super-imposition of several points of view to indicate total mental conception as opposed to partial direct vision. (Fourth dimensionalism.)

(5) Pictures created as *memoria,* objects and abstract design intermingled.

(6) Experiments in new materials and in *three* dimensions.*
(This phase seems to have been stimulated by a desire to push research beyond the limits of painting.   It was quickly discontinued.)

(7) Development of pure pattern and colour containing space suggestion.

(8) Reduction of painting to two dimensions ; space suggestions eliminated.

Through all these changes the artist is but claiming one thing. He claims the right, which the poet has already, to take an object into his mind, to ponder over it, to reshape it according to his

* *Plank Art* (Wyndham Lewis).

emotion, and to remake it into an original work of art ; something which is a creation of the artist's particular consciousness.   He is, strange though it may seem, keeping strictly within the limits of Ruskin's definition, he is describing nature.   He is describing nature with a liberty similar to that which Keats has claimed :

> " As when upon a tranced summer-night
>   Those green-robed senators of mighty woods,
>   Tall oaks, branch-charmed by the earnest stars,
>   Dream, and so dream all night without a stir." *

But the nature which he is describing is no longer that external visible *appearance* which Ruskin held only permissible for description.   He describes nature fused and moulded by his instincts as a painter.   He is in fact describing man, who also is a " *work* of the Creator."

There is no doubt that Cubism and, indeed, modern art generally owes part of its rapid advance to elements which lie without the bounds of painting proper.   This external element is very visible in the development of Cubism, although that art claims to be the purest presentation of plastic form possible.   Cubism began as a painter's problem, but mixed with Cubism at its inception were two poets, Guillaume Apollinaire and André Salmon, and one mathematician, Monsieur Princet.   Apollinaire was an exotic poet avid of new sensations, nor can the exoticism of Salmon's earlier poetry be overlooked.   In his book on Cubism Apollinaire says that Picasso, though the greatest of the artists, would not have had the courage to push his experiments far in the face of public disapprobation.

* It will be seen that all the poet's descriptions, tranced, green-robed senators, etc., are not only *not* descriptions, but are impossible when applied to the objects to which they actually are attached.   We can only understand the words by taking them out of the context and imagining them in a new plane of existence.   We have become almost subconsciously capable of making this mental leap, but Lafcadio Hearn gives an instance that the Japanese cannot understand the line, " She was more beautiful than day."   They cannot make the particular kind of psychological interchange necessary to connect the two ideas of beauty.   The *intellectual* appreciation of Cubism requires a mental effort of an analogous nature.

PICASSO
THREE NUDES

And, indeed, for a while Picasso did cease his experiments, allowing Braque to go forward. There is no doubt that the metaphysical and philosophical literature which launched Cubism owes its origin largely to Apollinaire, and perhaps some of the ideas to the intelligence of Derain, who is closely connected with the beginnings of Cubism.

The theories of the fourth dimension come obviously from abstract mathematics ill understood in a poet's or a painter's brain. It has indeed a fair seductive sound, probably as strange to its employers as their pictures were to the public. Fourth dimension is a definite mathematical abstraction and has nothing to do with art whatever, nor indeed can it be imagined by a painter who by his very gifts is the most bound of all persons to the three dimensions.

Apollinaire's lust for new artistic sensations became more marked when he urged Orphism on to Delaunay and assisted at the birth of the " *Disque solaire simultané*," which was at the beginning of the pell-mell of new " isms " which sprang up and died as rapidly as weeds during 1912, 1913, 1914.

Picasso—Pablo Ruiz is his real name—is the most vivid and the most dramatic personality which has come into the art of to-day. Born in Malaga, removed at the age of six to Barcelona where his father was a professor at the Academy of Arts, Picasso early showed signs of his progidious talent by carrying off a third prize at the Barcelona exhibition while he was only fourteen years old.

Picasso may well be considered as the problem of modern art. He has bewildered the public by the variety of and the differences between his artistic phases. An exhibition of haphazard Picassos, such as that held at the Leicester galleries, looks like the work of a group of five or six men who have scarcely an obvious idea between them. Monsieur Coquiot, the often subtly malicious author of " Les Indépendants," calls Picasso a chameleon and the epithet seems not unearned. Indeed, if one examines Picasso's career, the adjective has a peculiar appositeness. A chameleon not only changes colour, but it reflects the colour of its surroundings. Picasso, however, is a chameleon with some internal illuminant, he often reflects a borrowed colour more strongly than he has received it.

Picasso, as a young student fresh from Barcelona, began with an admiration for Steinlen. He painted Steinlens better than can Steinlen himself. Lautrec, Gauguin, and El Greco follow as inspirations. Puvis de Chavannes is added and then Cézanne.

To-day amongst the more advanced painters it is the fashion to decry Gauguin, and one must admit that Gauguin's peculiar vision, as I have pointed out, was that of a poet rather than that of a painter. Yet Gauguin held and was the first to propagate a series of truths which have been developed by the younger generation. Gauguin was the first to see that the practice of painting, or of plastic art generally, had become unnecessatily complex; that a painter could state truths simply. " A metre of green is more green than a centimetre if one wishes to express greenness." But nobody before Gauguin had wanted to express greenness. Most of the Fauves come in under the leadership of Gauguin's painting.

It is not curious that Picasso should have taken so eagerly to Cézanne, he was only returning to his native land. There is no doubt that Cézanne owed a great deal to the study of El Greco; there are portraits by Cézanne which are posed line for line from pictures by the Spanish Greek. It is natural too that El Greco has left an impress upon Spain. Malaga was the centre of a school of still-life painting which was most flourishing about the middle of the last century. This school concentrated upon the painting of fruity and luscious still lives to excite the Andalusian appetite. Many of the pictures of this school remind one of some of the lesser works of Cézanne, both in method of design and in manner of painting. It is possible that this school may in some way have developed from influences of El Greco. Picasso, thus, was in a way but going home, and his works of the Cézannesque period are extremely powerful.

Picasso at this time was associated with a group of men, all of whom have since made a mark in the world of Paris art. He was associated with Derain, Vlaminck, Braque, and Agero who were

PABLO PICASSO
THE RED CLOTH. (1922)

artists, with Max Jacob who stood straddling one leg in art and one in poetry, with Apollinaire and André Salmon, poets first, critics afterwards, but both avid of new sensations, with Princet, ingenious mathematician, who would explain the world by means of X's, Y's, and mathematical progressions to infinity. In this gathering one finds a collection of intelligences each of which can stimulate the other. Neither poet nor mathematician sees painting with the painter's eye, yet the ideas of both may react in enlarging the painter's idea. The poet may be prepared to advance towards logical conclusions which the painter may not be ready for. All these men were conscious of the enlargement of the boundaries of artistic thought which had been indicated by Seurat, Van Gogh, Gauguin, and Rousseau, and naturally their young and adventurous intelligences were curious to see how far these boundaries extended.

On the top of Cézannism came the realization of the value of the Negro art, which showed to what heights of emotional expression an extremely audacious and simplified art could reach. Picasso became more frankly Negro than any, but on to the Negro art he imposes further essays in Cézannism and certain technical devices used by Van Gogh. There is a period which wavered between Negroism with Cézanne impositions, and Cézannism with Negro simplifications. The latter phase of the two conquered, and Picasso arrived at the stage when he produced the pictures of Ebro, which Matisse dubbed " Cubist."

There is, of course, no doubt that many of the literary explanations of Cubism come from the fertile brain of Apollinaire, who from the first urged on the Cubist experiments. But in spite of this there is no question that Picasso is a very subtle and sensitive student of the mental processes. The painter who concentrates upon vision and the æsthetic quality naturally comes to problems in vision, in presentation, and in mental concepts which are very different from those held by ordinary men, but which I have shown were analysed by Galton before 1869.

Cézanne, in many of his pictures, had forced his sky into harmony with the spatial conception of his compositions, and in the Ebro designs Picasso deliberately continued his cubic designs into the sky portion of the picture. But he had not yet dared to desert realism.

I have heard that the first definite abstract composition, that is, a composition without a realistic, or descriptive intention, was evolved in this way. A Spanish sculptor named Agero was living in the same house as Picasso. This sculptor under Picasso's influence was designing some bas-reliefs on African models. Picasso got the idea that he could study the effects of space design more intensely by painting on to these reliefs with Cézannian emphasis. As Agero could not work fast enough, Picasso began to make bas-reliefs for himself, but out of cardboard, following the somewhat rigid shapes he had evolved in his Ebro and Negroid compositions. The final result he studied in various lights and from different angles and finally transferred to a flat canvas.

He was, however, a little timid of the results which he had reached; and it was his enthusiastic co-worker Braque who first faced the public with a truly Cubist composition at the Société des Indépendants of 1909.

From then onwards Picasso pressed Cubism farther and farther in different researches of spatial vision, *memoria*, and pure design. At first his compositions were indicated with a lack of colour and in a brown tonality, but gradually he reinforced the colour, until in 1920 his last Cubist designs are in frank and clear colouring.

During the excitement of Futurism, Picasso was dragged along with the crowd and tried a series of *outré* experiments with strange materials : pieces of wood, slips of newspaper, tram-tickets, and so on. I feel that to this phase of his effort one may apply the admirable motto of " Action." " It is better to try to go forward a step at the risk of making a mistake than to stay dully where one is with the surety of being right." Mistakes are quickly forgotten and over-looked by the world ; but the staying where one is is a block in the march of development.

Picasso's Cubism has definitely set the world's ideas of the art

G. BRAQUE
COMPOSITION

of painting upon a different basis. Even if Cubism at last proves too difficult an art to produce and to enjoy, the effects of Cubism upon the thoughtful artist must have a profound result on the art of the following centuries. Every art school should have a Cubist class, for a struggle with the problems of Cubism is a struggle with the fundamentals of the art of painting.

After a while Picasso tired of pursuing only the problems of non-representative form. He had tested the possibilities of Cézannism, Negroism, and metaphysical cubism, and his restless mind, looking for other kinds of adventure, found them in a new research following the Academism of Ingres. But even Ingres failed to satisfy him, and he has toyed with surrealism.

Although to Picasso we must ascribe practically all the important *conventions* of Cubism, including the guitar, the clay pipe, the false graining, the bottles of alcohol and the printed letters, yet we do not feel that Picasso's mind works quite at first hand. This man, the most original of the present day, always seems to evolve his originalities out of the ghost of some other painter. Perhaps, indeed, his concentrated studies of the art galleries have done Picasso as much harm as good.

Braque, who was the first exhibitor of an abstract picture, may be considered somewhat as the co-operator with and the codifier of Picasso. There is naturally, amongst the less inventive men, a tendency to form a school or an academy upon the experiments of original thinkers. This is especially the case during these days when the whole art world is in a sort of flux, and when new manifestation has followed new manifestation with bewildering rapidity. Thus, almost every phase of the development of Matisse has left behind a little group of disciples who, having come to understand the work of the artist at that moment, were too mentally exhausted, by the effort, to learn anything more and remain *sur place* repeating what they have learned over and over again. The ranks of art are, of course, overflowing with these parrot-like human beings, amongst whom are most of our fashionable portrait painters.

This does not mean that Braque is of the parrot tribe.   He may, perhaps, be considered as the real leader of the Cubist school.   But, to be a leader, one must possess some of the qualities of the led, the general recognizes the army discipline.   The man who disdains discipline can never be a general.   Thus Picasso cannot be considered as the *chef d'école* of the Cubists.   Picasso invents a convention, uses it twice and forgets all about it, in a new invention. Braque adopts the convention, turns it about, standardizes the convention, and presents it in a form in which it can be useful to all the disciples and parrots of the Cubist school.   For instance, amongst others the convention of the guitar, invented by Picasso, seems to become universal in the Cubist painting owing to the exertions of Braque.

Braque is a sombre and restrained painter who has a considerable power of presentation.   He is as disdainful of employing any seductive qualities in his work as Derain.   His colour schemes are based upon white, black, olive green, and khaki.   He uses his images with a pitiless logic.   Braque is a kind of Praise-God Barebones of Cubism ; or, he is the Quaker of Cubism.   Æsthetics are here carried beyond the sensual into the religious.

By about 1920 Braque came to an end of his pure cubism.   From 1920 to 1930 he uses a decorative convention, half abstract, half representative, principally based on a knife, a jug, a fruit dish, a few lemons, and so on.   From 1930 he follows Picasso into the metaphysical, but latterly has made a series of what look like planchette scrawls executed in a white line on black and tinged with Greek allusions.

Fernand Léger is the artist who most frankly accepts the world of mechanism towards which we appear to be tending.   He comes into Cubism later than Picasso and Braque, at first with some adaptation of the former methods.   However, he quickly differentiated himself, because of his concentration upon the mechanical aspect of things. Léger stimulates his imagination with machinery.   An aeroplane engine, a girder bridge, the signal discs of a railway station, and so

FERNAND LÉGER
STILL LIFE

on, are to him the highest forms of expression of the present century and, as he points out, often reach a quality of pure design which is supremely beautiful.

In his compositions he tries to get some of the rigidity of iron and the flexibility of steel. His pictures are carefully designed and full of a sort of harsh gaiety produced by strongly contrasting primitive colours taken straight from the tube ; a harsh gaiety which echoes the blare of the merry-go-round and the cacophonous discords of a mechanical fair.

There is an apt adaptation of his mechanical methods in his large picture of soldiers playing cards. It expresses vividly the base of modern war ; the reduction of men to the slaves of machinery, to be in the end moulded into a sort of awkward, unblenching machine themselves : the army machine.

Léger's tints are the gay tints with which we paint the motor-bus or the motor-car ; but one feels that this gaiety is but an exterior varnish over something immeasurably solemn. The throb of a motor is not a laugh, but a threat. This colouring has something sinister in it, and Léger's pictures often seem more gay in a photograph than they do in colour.

Léger has not deserted a sort of realism. Even his most abstract compositions are founded upon shapes and objects which come from the mechanical world : signal discs, steel pillars, and so on. He recently seems to be more and more tempted back to a sort of fierce mechanical reality. He believes in joy, but it must be something of the joy of the machine which catches a man's arm in its teeth or the laugh of a rushing engine belt which whirls a workman off to destruction. Léger is the leading artist of the sixth stage of Cubism. He is also, after Picasso, perhaps, the most original and inventive of the Cubist school.

At the beginning Gleizes slipped into Cubism more slowly than did his confrères. His first essays are more in the nature of bold simplification of forms with insistence upon spatial compositions. But, making haste with leisure, Gleizes comes at last to be the leader

L

of the most advanced artist school; a school so advanced, indeed, that it ceases to be Cubist in any way.

The Cubists have not languished for lack of literary explanation, but Gleizes has written his own act of faith in a book called *Cubism and the Means of Understanding It*. We may suspect most purely literary explanations; poets are not painters and are easily misled, one only penetrates a craft by practising it. But Gleizes is a painter, and we can therefore quote Gleizes's own definitions of his art:

" Painting is the art of giving life to a flat surface. A flat surface exists only in two dimensions. It is *true* only in two dimensions.

" To pretend to give it a third dimension, is to make it deny its own nature.

" Painting should be in two dimensions : only sculpture has three.

" A work of art is a concrete spiritual manifestation. In the exterior world only the physical aspect of an object strikes us. The spirit is hidden, mysterious, and we have to make an effort to reveal it.

" In a work of art it is only the spirit which should be visible. The physical aspect is hidden and mysterious and we must struggle to find it.

" Painting therefore is not an imitation of things.

" The reality of the exterior world serves us as a point of departure, but art strips off the realism to reveal the spirit.

" Setting out from that which is temporary it reaches towards the infinite."

Gleizes lives up to his profession; he is at the last and seventh stage. He now composes pictures which are purely geometrical in form, filled in with flat, harmonized, and clean colours, without modelling or space suggestions other than those made by the juxtapositions of the flat tints.

But one feels that this manifesto tends to deny things which are obvious truths. The suggestion of the third dimension, depth, on a flat surface has an emotional value, especially when the flat surface is not denied. The presentation of the physical aspect of objects does not impede the revelation of the spirit.

ALBERT GLEIZES
FIGURE-TEMPERA

We are not trying to deny that great works of art may not be painted in two dimensions; but we wish to deny the value of exclusive theory in creating works of art. Art, as we have said before, depends solely on the artist. Giotto could have made works of art out of anything, he could have broken any laws with impunity.

With Gleizes, Cubism pursues its way to a logical development. This art of abstract flat surfaces of coloured shapes is an art which, in its way, can reach to the highest points of pictorial purity. It is parallel with the music of the tone poem from which all melody is banished. There is, however, a further development of this abstract painting which I foresee. This is an art of moving shapes and colour, produced by some process akin to the cinema. This art, which has been hinted at in some modern dramatic productions, still needs the artist who can employ its possibilities. An art of moving abstract colour and form would place painting upon the same footing as music. At present the painting of Gleizes appears to me an arrested moment in a colour-form symphony which has no beginning and no end.

Metzinger is the only Cubist remaining to-day. That is to say, he is the only one who clings to the Cézannian dictum that " Nature can be expressed by the cube, the cone, and the cylinder. Anyone who can paint these simple forms can paint nature." Metzinger might more properly be called a Cubo-Realist. Occasionally he leans over towards Braqueism and the mental juggle of objects and abstract pattern, but usually his experiments are of a quite simple nature, tinged with a flavour of sentimentalism which sits queerly upon the lofty and brooding spirit of the Cubist.

Herbin is the most hardy colourist of the original Cubist school. He is also the most persistent seeker for novel effects. If we remember the simile of the chemist which I made use of in Chapter XIII., Herbin has already made up some hundreds of mixtures without seeming to be satisfied that the philosopher's stone is at the bottom of any one. Herbin has no formula; he has, on the contrary, a good instinct for decoration and for colour which make even his most advanced experiments pleasantly plausible.

—— André Lhote stands midway between Cubism and Realism. He may be considered as the intellectual painter *par excellence*. He reasons not only in paint, but in words, and with eloquent prose he reveals the intellectual processes of his past and future development in a series of brilliant articles which have appeared in *La Nouvelle Revue française*, some of which have been translated for the *Athenæum*. Lhote shows how Picasso is the logical explanation of Cézanne and of Ingres; Lhote himself is a similar explanation of Picasso.

In his painting one feels the presence of the subtle and logical reasoner, and he shows us the numbers of drawings and studies by means of which he arrives at each result. He wishes to perform no artist's legerdemain. There is something very admirable in the clear precision of Lhote's artistic statement. It is the direct negation of all that the Impressionists taught, and even of much that Cézanne held. It may be considered, I think, a more difficult task to be clear than to be suggestive. The suggestive picture allows the spectator to supply much of his own feeling; if the form is indecisive the spectator can conceive an ideal form within the indecision. But the artist who is formal and precise binds us down to his own thought. The more precise in his form, the more he must have pondered upon its exactness, more clearly are his errors visible, if errors he makes.

It is for this reason that often the sketch by a second-rate artist pleases us more than his completed picture. For in the latter he has attempted precision without the capacity to conceive a form perfect enough for precision.

It is, also, more difficult for the spectator to enjoy a precise form than a suggestive one. The spectator must be prepared to submit himself completely to the artist, he must be content to accept the artist's thoughts. If he tries to add his own he finds they cannot be contained by this particular work of art; and so we often hear the

METZINGER

LANDSCAPE

artist who strives for precise and insuggestive form is accused of coldness. Naturally this accusation has been levelled against Lhote.

Lhote's mind is analytic to a high and subtle degree; his articles on Cézanne and on Ingres exhibit this quality, and this analysis is naturally very evident in his painting. Even in his most abstract work he believes in presenting an image of the natural sources from which he drew the idea, he produces thus a sort of realism founded upon a Cubist structure.

The illustrations to this chapter have been chosen in order to give, as it were, a cross-section of the development of Cubism. Each *illustration* can be taken to represent a different stage. Thus:

1st stage. Metzinger (cubic-realism).
2nd stage. Herbin (nature reduced to cubic pattern).
3rd stage. Braque (*memoria*, letters and abstract design).
4th stage. Léger (mechanisms).
5th stage. Picasso (spatial abstract design).
6th stage. Gleizes (flat abstract design).

This does not imply that each artist illustrated stops short of this stage. Herbin, for instance, has ranged at will over all of the varied manifestations; so has Picasso.

CHAPTER XV

THE MODERN REALISTS

A WELL-KNOWN painter once gave his frame-maker a ticket for an art exhibition. The artisan was an oldish man who had been in the trade for many years, and who had shown a certain taste in fitting his frames to pictures. Some of his naïve criticisms had delighted the painter, so when the old man returned from the exhibition his opinion was demanded with some curiosity.

" A shoddy lot," returned the frame-maker. " A shoddy lot, sir."

" Bless my soul, you don't think so ! " exclaimed his patron. " But some of the pictures are by Masters."

" Pictures ! " answered the old man, " why, I didn't look at the pictures. I'm talking about the frames."

In a similar way artists tend to go through life looking at the frame, and ignoring the picture. Nature is the frame of life. It is only the foursquare which makes a limiting edge around the boundaries of experience. If we continue to consider only the frame of nature, ignoring the emotional content, we are on the same level as the old frame-maker. If we allow ourselves to smile at him, at the same time we smile at ourselves.

We have to-day realized that there may be a mental distinction between the frame and the picture which it encloses, or between the straightforward or photographic vision of life and the emotional content which is stimulated by vision. In painting, the presentation of the emotional content—which is the language of the painter's

AUGUSTE HERBIN
THE PONT-NEUF

spirit—is more important than the exhibition of his study or of his accuracy. In spite of Ruskin's proof of the superior knowledge of Turner over Claude, we turn with more delight to the latter's pictures than to those of the former. Doubtless Turner exercised a very commendable though second-rate novelist's intelligence in putting children playing with boats in the foreground of his " Building of Carthage " ; but, when one is carried away by the magic of a great artist's creation, one does not want to be disturbed by trivialities of such a nature ; they show the very opposite of what Ruskin was trying to prove. In the conception of the building of Carthage the importance and magnificence should have been solved by weight and line and colour, by artistic means alone and not by incident.

Let us imagine a scene in a public park upon a summer Sunday afternoon. The painter has had a good lunch with perhaps wine not too obviously manufactured. He feels at peace with his fellow-men. The Sunday crowds upon the grass amuse him, even the vulgar music of the band chimes in with his mood. *But*, if he has had a bad meal, if something has disagreed with him, if the Chianti was logwood, the people will seem vapid, the sun too hot, the children exasperating, the band hideous. Thus, we see that the same frame contains two pictures which are very different. And these two pictures do not depend upon external vision, but upon internal chemistry.

The *trained* painter would merely imitate the scene, copying his tints from nature as well as he could ; the modern realist would be trying to create a reflection of his personal reactions to the scene, he would be *studying himself*. This second task needs a higher capacity than the former. With a little perseverance, at least three-quarters of humanity can be taught to paint from nature ; or rather can be taught that particular convention of art which is called painting from nature. But it is impossible to teach anyone how to transcribe himself. This can be called indeed " creation." It is either comparatively easy or quite impossible ; artists are born, not made—

though a born artist may be destroyed by bad training or influence. Easy, of course, does not mean careless ; little good painting is done without considerable thought.   The task of creating in one's mind an image which does not exist in nature involves a mental effort of a very different nature from that easy one of adopting images directly from the nature which is before you.   This art of transposition, of the infusion of nature with a spiritual meaning, is carried to the highest point by the Chinese and Japanese artists.   We have in Western art no painters who approach the Eastern in spiritual conception.

In attempting to escape from the obsession of nature, the Cubists tried to carve their thoughts out of shape and colour alone.   But there are a good many gifted painters who are not prepared to desert nature altogether.   They realize that art is only a language, and that it is more easy to be understood, and perhaps more natural to speak in a dialect which is more generally intelligible.

They can, also, be considered as being more in harmony with their age, since the day has not yet come when man has completely imposed himself upon nature.   Perhaps the day for Cubism will be the one when man has created synthetic Foods and mineral cloths.   At all events, Cubism, though in its infancy, has failed to become popular, and its place has been taken by those who profess pure abstraction or psycho - analytical surrealism.   The group of painters of whom we now are treating have been mingled with the Fauves, but gradually their younger experiences have solidified into the divergent techniques which are illustrated here.

In the early part of the book I have tried to develop the ideas of harmonic structure of a picture, and naturally these painters concentrate upon the same qualities and in them these qualities are remarkable, although expressed in different aspects.   We might, perhaps, invent some tabulating method of getting over the ground more quickly.   We might sum each one up by a formula, by a series of categories, allowing each category a possible total of ten good marks—like the schoolboy's exercise.

MARIA BLANCHARD
THE CHILD ON THE STEPS

Thus :

Monsieur A. B.

    Linear design . . . 7 (angular)
    Colour harmony . . 5 (tending towards coolness and monotony)
    Spatial design . . . 8
    Emotional intensity . 7

But it would make art criticism even drier reading then it is to-day.

These artists whom we would not insult by summing up in so frigid a method are the essential founders of the modern movements. If we have singled out Derain and Vlaminck for another chapter, it is not because these other men are less important than the late école du Chatou, but merely because Derain and Vlaminck were useful to my purpose in illustrating certain problems of latter-day art. Friesz, Dufy, and Van Dongen were exhibitors at the Independents before either Derain or Vlaminck appeared, and each one pursues a line of personal development at least as interesting as that pursued by any of the others.

There has been of late amongst painters a tendency to colour the frame in order to suit the picture, and we find in accordance with this spirit that the Royal Academy has withdrawn its ban on coloured frames. But this habit of choosing the frame is of comparatively recent importance. The original function of art was to decorate architecture. That is, the frame was first made, and the picture had to be conceived to suit the frame. The picture was subordinate to the architecture, and this branch of the painter's art is still rightly considered as the most difficult and the highest achievement when successfully carried out. We may find that the task of the modern realist is analagous to that of the fresco or decorative painter. The decorative painter will use the lines of the architecture, that is, of the frame, as a structure for his picture, but his picture need not be strictly architectural. The rigid lines of the architecture will be eased off, counter-balanced, and so on. The modern realist will use the lines of his subject, that is, of nature, as structure for his picture, but he will not necessarily be tied to nature. The decorator must consider the lines, design, and character of his building. It would have been as foolish to have placed a Gothic design in the panels of the Panthéon, as the actual panel of Meissonier or that of Laurens is foolish. Puvis de Chavannes was the only one of the artists decorating the Panthéon who realized that for a psuedo-Greek building the only possible decoration must be in a pseudo-Greek manner.

In a similar way the modern realist considers his pictorial structure in harmony with his subject. If we want to give a name to this kind of harmonization, we might say that he is making a " pictorial paraphrase " of his subject. It is clear that a paraphrase may be an expanded or a contracted one. In general one may say that the tendency of to-day is allied to that of the old Japanese poets. It is a tendency to reduce the paraphrase to brilliant yet, in its way, complete brevity. Some people imagine that it is easier to be brief than to be loquacious. They would imagine that it is easier to paint a Dufy than to paint a Meissonier. These persons can only admire external evidences of almost thoughtless labour ; they are unable to admire internal evidences of an equally extended labourless thought.

Dufy is one of the most vivid of the modern draughtsmen. His drawings have an élan, a delicacy of sensation comparable only to the line drawings of Picasso. In painting, Dufy presents, perhaps, one of the most forcible illustrations of the restlessness which modern developments have forced upon the intellectual artist. Dufy is conscious of what must be shaped by the artist, but has often been somewhat irresolute as to the means by which this product may be reached.

Dufy seems always to be straining paint to explain his thought. He visualizes in similes ; for instance, he sees the sea like a parquet, and in a series of pictures he insists upon this comparison. Dufy is, perhaps, an *imagier* rather than an analyst, he is allied in mentality

RAOUL DUFY
SYRACUSE. (WATER-COLOUR)

to the Russian school, which we will discuss later. He is a decorator and designer with a strong affiliation to the processes and the simplifications of the early wood-cutters.

I have already compared the work of Dufy to that of the Japanese poets. We find here the same anxiety to reduce a statement of impression to the simplest of facts. Allied to this is a disposition which we have already noted in Chapter III. The simple man whom I there described drawing a bucket mixes up visual impressions with acquired knowledge, and produces a drawing which is a compound of both. But the man who becomes conscious of these two aspects of the mental understanding of things has an equal right to combine the mental and visual conceptions, only his combination is conscious, explanatory, and selected. The simpler man's is *naïveté ;* the conscious man's is essentially the opposite of naïve, although it presents at first sight a naïve appearance. Dufy uses this right, and his paintings, which may to some appear like the productions of the nursery, are in fact the result of careful selection, elimination, and simplification.

Like the ancient wood-cutters and the sculptors of the Assyrian monuments, Dufy attempts no deceptive perspective, nor any imitation of third dimension or depth. The æsthetic quality of his work depends principally upon pattern, while the emotional quality is derived from a sub-conscious descriptive force.

The common method of attack against modern art is to assume that the artists are either ignorant or impertinent, or lazy. French criticism, on the other hand, accuses Jean Marchand of being too careful, too learned in the picture galleries. Marchand is, perhaps, one of the most conscientious painters of the day. In this he is allied to Derain, as he is also allied to Derain and Segonzac, by his repudiation of seductive colour. One rarely feels with Marchand that a gust of emotion tempted him to do something banal as it sometimes tempts Vlaminck ; one rarely feels that anything has been overlooked—every line, every space, seems to be reflected over and shaped. Sometimes Marchand produces a design which is almost grotesque, sometimes one which appears quite *ordinary*, but one feels that both grotesqueness and ordinariness have been deliberate.

Marchand represents, perhaps, the most direct development of the Cézannian theory of composition. For a while he experimented with a sort of mosaic Cubism beneath his realism : but essentially Marchand represents the new Cézanne academism controlled by conscious constructive imagination.

Friesz, though he resembles neither, lies about half-way between the extremes of Derain and Vlaminck. He has an energy more controlled than that of Vlaminck and therefore more varied and inventive ; he has an imagination more exuberant than that of Derain. One may find his origins in Gauguin, his development through Cézanne, and also through some of the old Flemish painters.

To understand clearly the methods of spatial construction, combined with linear design, which characterises the modern realists, one can do nothing better than study a series of canvases of Friesz. His compositions have a clarity and a logic which, however, is usually in complete accord with the subject of his picture. In certain of his canvases painted before Cubism was evolved there are already indications of a regulated sense of space which might have tempted him to develop a Cubism of his own. But there is a lyrical spirit in Friesz which prevented him from attempting abstraction. Perhaps, like Van Gogh, he had a terror of losing form. Nor does Friesz scorn what is sometimes contemptuously called " Illustration "—that is, the portrayal of an idea, which may be partly literary in conception.

Literature in picture-making is harmful as long as it takes the principal place with the spectator. As long as Lamb can discuss the " Barrenness of the Imaginative Faculty in production of Modern Art " from the standpoint in which he does, or as long as Ruskin can praise Turner for his literary ingeniousness, so long is literature dangerous to the artist. If all record of Dido or of Carthage were lost and forgotten from men's brains, the picture by Turner would

A. DUNYOER DE SEGONZAC

A SPRING LANDSCAPE

have to stand upon its pictorial merits, and its children sailing boats would be meaningless.

But Friesz keeps his illustration in its proper place : he is first of all a constructor and a sensitive painter ; secondly, his brush travels with a nervous vitality which expresses clearly the close intercommunication of brain and hand.

The academic artist takes it for granted that the modern artist denies the value of the past. Because *he* is an imitation of the past, and because the modern artist denies *him*, therefore the modern artist denies the past. But the modern artist does not deny the past ; he only denies miscomprehensions and echoes of the past. He would deny a man who mispaints Rembrandt and claims it as original art, as he would deny a man who misquotes Shakespeare and claims it as a new valuable poetic production. First-hand art is the only art of value, because first-hand life is the only life of value ; and every new manifestation of life is a unique and original manifestation. History never repeats itself. We can imagine no more absurd character of fiction than that of a young man who sedulously sets out to be a copy of his father, who imitates his father's virtues and vices, and who chooses his bride because of a likeness to his mother. Yet such ideal is held up before Art Students, and it is the ideal which still governs much contemporary criticism.

Segonzac is one of the younger artists who most clearly show their ancestry, without in any way being for that an imitative development. He is like the son of an ancient house in whom some physical family trait comes out with startling distinctness, without affecting his naturally developed character. Segonzac is, perhaps, one of the few modern artists who might have been painting in the same style had Cézanne and the Impressionists not existed. There is an intimate liaison between him and the Fontainebleau school of French landscape. But Segonzac owes to modern thought, first, his tremendous concentration upon the architecture and design of his compositions ; secondly, the curious use he makes of his qualities of sheer paint, creating spatial suggestion by means of his surfaces. Like Derain, like Dufresne, Segonzac also represents the new protest against the flood of badly organized colour which has overwhelmed painting.

Dufresne is another reaction against loose and inexpressive colouring. In fact, because of the sombre quality of his work, owing to the subtlety of his contrasts of deep siennas, reds, blacks, and ochres, it has been extremely difficult to find a suitable picture for reproduction in half-tone. This artist represents a point which lies somewhat parallel with that of Dufy, but more subjected to Cubism and therefore more modelled and moulded in sensation.

Dufresne illustrates an aspect of painting which we have not yet mentioned. If one takes the trouble to analyse the work of most painters, one finds that their pictures are constructed upon a sinuous linear interweaving of the lines of shapes and of silhouettes. Often this line can be followed flowing in and out continuously through a series of movements which constitute what has been called the " Rhythm " of the picture. Pushed to its farthest extreme this linear flow of line can be called " Arabesque." In Friesz especially one discovers this interweaving of linear movement, and again in Lhote it is very easily perceived. But another kind of harmony can be set up in painting. This is a harmony of balanced spaces rather than a harmony of interweaving outlines. In such a harmony the objects of the pictures tend to be separated, and one feels amongst them a mutual interplay of shape and spaces which are themselves of beautiful and pleasing form. The first kind of composition is produced by mutually interflowing lines, the second by interacting boundaries. In a musical analogy the first would be played *legato*, the second *staccato*.

Both Dufresne and Dufy tend to this *staccato* type of composition. Naturally one never finds this quality quite separated from the other; the composer in Arabesque seeks to vary his compositions by means of interacting silhouettes, the composer in silhouette strengthens his construction with a few architectural lines.

DUFRESNE
THE HUNTER

Van Dongen is the Toulouse-Lautrec of to-day. He is the antithesis to Roualt, that savage painter of the nude. Van Dongen is the artist of " La Vie Parisienne " raised to a high point; he is the soul brother of Utamaro. George Moore is the only writer in the English language who could adequately transcribe Van Dongen into prose.

Van Dongen combines sensuality, grace, and style, and therefore is a proper product of one aspect of modern Parisian life. He is daring in his liberties with nature; and successful owing to his peculiar self-confidence; often vulgar, he is rarely banal, and his compositions are usually complete and striking. Even when he paints landscapes his success seems to come from a sensuality which betrays itself both in line and in colour. Van Dongen is allied to Matisse in his purely technical researches, though Matisse has shown more courage in colour research. It is curious that the most Parisian painter of French women should be a Dutchman.

Van Dongen has developed the technical method of the Japanese wood-cutters. He indicates his colours often only by the edge, and produces in this way decorative effects which are very striking. His later works have lost much of the peculiar power of his earlier pictures. Like Vlaminck he tends to repeat himself too often, but his conventions are not so varied as those of Vlaminck. Van Dongen seems to have a tendency nowadays to go back not to nature for inspiration, but to Van Dongen. This creates a vicious circle which limits the painter's powers instead of expanding them.

The modern Realistic school is that which to-day is gaining ground and strength more than its rival, the Cubist, non-representative school. And, indeed, upon analysis the former conforms most nearly to the present stage of civilization. I am afraid that Cubism in art must lie on a level with ideals in politics; universally possible only with a re-created humanity—it is, in fact, the art of Utopia.

I have limited this review of the modern realistic artists to those who are, in a way, the leading examples of various personal developments which, however, more or less cover the space between the realism of the last epoch and the Cubism of this.   This does not by any means exhaust the list of interesting, vigorous, and vital painters now in France.   Only space and expense prevents me from adding examples of Boussingault, Bissiere, De la Fresnay, Favory, Gondoin, Lotiron, Moreau, Mortier, Pascin, Vallotton, Waroquier and others who have contributed personal developments within the limits of the new French tradition.

VAN DONGEN
THE DRESSING-ROOM

CHAPTER XVI

THE SLAVONIC INFLUENCE

THE modern French developments in Art have practically absorbed the efforts of all other European countries. The Germans have received a side twist through the influence of the powerful but somewhat rhetorical Swiss painter Hodler and the Norwegian Munch, but in essence of their development they are Gauguinian and Picassian; Italy, in spite of the bombast of her Futurism, is dominated by French art, at second-hand, mixed with sentimentalism; Spain is represented by Picasso, who is now as French as a Frenchman; while the English artists of interest are all more or less under the direct influence of the various French developments. The attempts to create national art nowadays result only in producing art which is nationalistic, that is, possessing mannerisms without basis, like a cockney dressed up as a halberdier for a Lord Mayor's Show. The only country which contrived to retain a character of her own is Russia and the Slavonic lands generally, and this comes about because Russia long retained a national culture, and drew the sources of that culture from origins different from our own. The Russian * school has, it is true, submitted to the influence of the French, but it remained distinctive nevertheless, like a Tartar who has accepted the costume of civilization.

The Russian school is dominated by two factors : the peasant feeling for applied art, and the practice of Icon painting, which is a direct descendant from Byzantine decoration. We who live in the

* This refers particularly to the Moscow school; that of Petrograd is not interesting.

heterogeneous interiors to which bad taste, no taste, and manufactured taste have condemned us, can scarcely realize what it means to have been brought up in the midst of surroundings which have a uniform character and which belong to a national and therefore natural scheme of decoration. We cannot realize what it meant to be a Gothic, or an Egyptian, or a Greek, nor can we realize what it means to be a Russian.

The influence of Slavonic household art shows immediately when the Slav sets himself to painting. Roughly speaking, the Slavonic school possesses in the highest degree in Europe the power of colour as design. Even in great French colourists, such as Cézanne and Renoir, one finds that the beauty of the colour is a general beauty of interharmonized tints. If one stands so far away from a Renoir that all detail disappears one finds that the colour is distributed in vague patches, which are usually pleasing, but which are not very definitely organized into what one can call pattern.

This power of colour design has of course struck the public in the Russian Ballets ; and two of the artists responsible for much of the decoration of those ballets are characteristic of the qualities of the Slavonic school. These are Larianoff and Madame Gontcharova. These two artists exhibit the quality of colour used as design, of colour used as spatial and an emotional value, a research which the ex-Cubist Gleizes is trying to reduce to its simplest terms. Colour alone in painting may be considered as capable of an expansion almost musical in its complexity, and analagous to music in its psychological workings. Aristotle saw a likeness between colour harmonies and musical chords, and further researches have shown that the likeness is very deep rooted. We may recall the experimental colour organ of Mr. Rutherford, upon which he played symphonies in colour, from musical scores as if upon an organ. Scriabin suggested using this *visual* instrument in connection with an orchestra. One may divide up the colour circle into twelve notes : yellow, orange-yellow, orange, orange-red, red, red-violet, violet, violet-blue, blue, blue-green, green, green-yellow—and so back to

LARIANOFF

DECORATION FOR STAGE SETTING. (WATER-COLOUR)

yellow again, and one will find that approximately these notes behave like the musical notes. One can produce harmonies and discords in a like manner.

Now, if with this idea of harmonization and inter-relation of colours we examine any picture, we shall find that the artists' idea of colour " architecture " is often very rudimentary, even amongst the greatest masters. There have been as few great colourists as there have been few great comic writers. If under this colour scrutiny we analyse even that masterpiece of emotional colour, Titian's " Ariadne," we find that the colour distribution as pattern is almost bad in spite of the exquisite beauty of individual tints : the colour pattern of a picture such as Turner's " Temeraire " is very weak.

By *colour* one does not imply that actual colour must be forced to any exaggerated pitch of garishness. *Colour* covers every kind of tint, and every shade of grey. But intelligent colour realizes both the value of the most forceful as well as of the most subtle of notes. The colourist organizes his colour design as carefully as he organizes his linear or spatial construction. He uses colour according as it is *necessary to the emotional intention of his work.*

The second quality which stands out in the Slavonic school is the heritage from the Byzantine which comes through the Greek Church and through Icon painting. In this art the artist can consider personages and objects as symbols rather than as representation ; the symbol must be made recognizable, and once this necessity has been fulfilled the artist may take what liberties he likes. This does not release the artist from the necessity of creating those inherent constructions of line, space, and so on, but it liberates him from having either to consider or to overcome the temptations of realistic drawing. Chagall may be considered as the pre-eminent representative of this element of Slavonic art, although it is keenly present in the work of Gontcharova and Larianoff, as well as in that of the extremely versatile Madame Vassilieff. Chagall carries his symbolism so far that, if he wishes to show a horse which is in foal, he paints an image of the foal within the mare's womb ; a cow which is being carried to the slaughter-house he paints blue to indicate the emotional significance of the animal. Chagall's world can be considered as a world in which form and colour are subdued to a mystical meaning, a world of dreams in which anything is reasonable and everything logical.

Gontcharova and Marie Vassilieff represent the woman's side of Slavonic art. In spite of the supposed subjectivity of the feminine, both have passed through French influence, both have used Cubism ; without, however, allowing their personality to be subdued by the influence of either Picasso or Léger, or Gleizes. Vassilieff's compositions show with especial clarity the Slavonic sense of image surviving a long training in French schools of thought.

In coming to Polish painters we still find a definite indication of the influence of a bringing up under national conditions, although Poland may be considered as the merging ground of Western and Slavonic cultures. The Polish painters, Kisling and Madame Reno, are more markedly influenced by Western thought than the Russians. They can be included almost as examples of that international school of artistic thought which has grown up out of the recent French developments. Yet both of these painters show that Slavonic sensibility to colour as a compositional value in itself, while Madame Reno contrives by means of expedients, such as the one illustrated of a shop sign, to give reign to that sense of imagery which is so Slavonic a characteristic. Kisling is one of the most daring and brilliant of the colourists of the younger school, combining the imaginative and descriptive form of the modern realists with a Slavonic sense of lyric colour.

It is needless to say that the Slavonic school has been profoundly affected by the movements of Paris. It has borrowed liberally from, become conscious and organized with, its teachers. But at the same time one must consider that the inclusion of this spot of strongly characterized foreign culture within the Salon d'Automne and the Salon des Indépendants has had a returning effect upon French painting. The Slavonic imagery harmonized with and fortified the

MARIE LAURENCIN
PAINTING

Galerie Paul Rosenberg

folk-speech of Henri Rousseau ; and helped forward the simplifica-tion of drawing and directness of statement. The colour simplifica-tions of Gontcharova and others have had an undoubted influence upon the work of the modern realists. Even the Slavonic lack of humour and aptitude for pushing logic sometimes to absurdity, may have been useful in creating natural and healthy reactions. The Russian Ballet has had a tremendous influence upon the stage, and through the stage upon social life, and so upon the public attitude in general towards the modern developments in art. Indeed, I think that we may trace half of the public's advance towards the appreciation of modern art to the leaven of the Russian Ballet.

CHAPTER XVII

AFTER THE CUBISTS

A FAVOURITE accusation levelled by the Academics against the Moderns is that they have brutally broken with the past and that they have thrown overboard all tradition. The answer to that charge must depend entirely on whether one is tempted to take the long or the short view of what is implied by the word "tradition." We may justly say that Greek Art broke with Egyptian tradition, Gothic with Byzantine and Renaissance with Gothic. But here the Academics might be tempted to interpose that in breaking with the Gothic tradition Renaissance Art was but renewing allegiance with and carrying on Greek tradition, and so, although it was breaking with one tradition it returned to another which promised far more chances of development.

The argument is true enough. Renaissance Art did break with Gothic tradition to renew allegiance with the Greek. But if this was not a breach of tradition, we cannot exactly say that modernistic Art has wholly discarded tradition with a capital " T." It has actually discarded the observational-recording tradition developed from the Classic Greek Renaissance.

What modernistic development has done is rather to review, re-test and adapt to its own uses the virtues of almost every kind of æsthetic tradition of note that has existed since historical times. It has investigated the Chinese, the Indian, the Persian, the African, the South Sea Islanders, the Minoan, the Sumerian, the Etruscan and a number of other Arts that flourished in bygone days. Picasso has been, in a way, the greatest stock-taker who has ever forced the world to review the validity of what it displayed with so much self-satisfaction on its æsthetic counters. He has rummaged the attics

166

RENO

SIGN FOR A MILLINER'S SHOP

of the past, has brought out and refurbished old devices and has shown that they still have both vitality and validity. In consequence, the intelligent artist of to-day is left, not with the mere ruins of a broken tradition about him, but such a complicated wealth of ideas and means that the difficulty is to know what to do with them. He is almost swamped by his resources. In consequence, we see many a contemporary artist deliberately limiting himself to a narrow field of effort in order to avoid facing the terrifying complexity of the whole problem.

On the occasion of this third revision of a book which, first written in 1922, and though bearing marks of its date, still seems to be serving its purpose, I am tempted to answer one of the criticisms levelled against it. This was that in the course of my exposition I introduced, without attempting to judge between them, a number of forms of artistic endeavour which seemed in essence quite contradictory. It is true that many of the artists here illustrated are contradictory in spirit. It may be useful, even at the risk of repetition, to give a summary of those who have had most to do with the developments of the modernistic idiom.

IMPRESSIONISTS. Study of objects bathed in light and atmosphere and analysis of the artist's reactions in methods of suggestion.

CÉZANNE. Realization of solid form by means of colour. Composition by means of space suggestions and angular recession. Drawing distorted for compositional purposes.

RENOIR. Rhythmical composition of rounded forms and movement emphasized by light, sensuous coordination of colour.

SEURAT. Intensification of design by constructive logic and (with Signac) intensification of luminosity by pointillism.

GAUGUIN.   Deliberate simplification of contour and of colour areas. Research for the unusual in design.

VAN GOGH.   Intensification of emotional response by heightened visual impact of subject-matter. Exacerbated technique. Drawing distorted for emotional emphasis.

MATISSE.   The deliberately simplified vision. Intellectual research, under Oriental influence, for unusual design. Composition by colour spaces.

ROUSSEAU.   The simple mind gifted with the power to express itself with unabashed sincerity. Descriptive drawing.

MODIGLIANI.   Expression of human character by means of deliberate simplifications and overstatements.

PICASSO.   The adventurous mind with metaphysical tendencies. Almost every avenue explored, from realism to abstraction.

BRAQUE.   The adventurous logical mind. Cubism developing from discreet decoration to an apparently automatic linear shorthand.

LÉGER.   The mechanistic mind. Pattern and drawing reduced to the arts of the T-square and compass. Undiluted and often deliberately clashing colours.

To any one who examines this catalogue the contradictions must at once be obvious. Cézanne called Van Gogh a madman to his face. Renoir hardly fits in with, say, Braque, nor Modigliani with Leger ; Matisse and Rousseau, though both after simplicity, find it by very different routes. Yet a reference to pages 132 and 133 will show that in Art such contradictions do not invalidate the argument. They are not only possible but inevitable. Beauty, like a centre of gravity, admits of many " perpendiculars " which need not imply parallels but can assimilate diametric contradictions.

The truth is that theory can never make the artist. If the artist is of the class A, of which I have already spoken, he usually paints regardless of theory, driven by an irresistible impulse to express what is in him, and his methods grow out of his spiritual needs. The critic fits him out with a theory as the tailor fits his body with a suit of clothes. And since he is presumed to be an original artist, that is to say, one who has something to say that has not been said before, he will be forced to invent new methods of giving his message. This seems to be inevitable in a world of individuals, amongst whom Art is not subjected to some imperative cultural domination as it was during the earlier epochs.

And so I am bringing this study to a close with Cubism and its derivative Abstractionism because, with these two phases, the technical revolution of the twentieth century comes to a logical end. One cannot go far beyond flat abstract design in which there is no representation of objects nor any attempt at inducing the illusion of a third dimension. The motto set up over the portals of the æsthetic Abbaye de Thélème is the old one of " Fais ce que voudras," and who can want more liberty than that.

After a half-century of struggle the artist has won a grudging agreement to his claim that to the province of Art belongs practically any kind of mark humanly made on any other surface (painting) or any kind of a lump of stuff deliberately shaped into any other kind of a lump (sculpture). This is not put satirically. Art does begin to come in as soon as a human being determines to change something else in order to increase its beauty, its significance or its emotional content. To what extent he increases these elements does not depend on the means he uses, nor on what methods he selects, nor, in other words, on what school of æsthetic thought he belongs to, but only to his personal and individual power as an artist. In fact, " Fais ce que voudras," to which should be added " Quality must tell."

If artists themselves would only leave it there all would be well, but, unfortunately, different schools of thought in Art assume all the arrogances of different forms of thought in religion. To each school there is but one way to Salvation, its own. So having won a full liberty of action the world of Art actually remains prisoner, with each school firmly shut in its own cell and growling at its neighbours through its self-imposed bars.

Having won this liberty, Art paused for a moment to recover from the shock of the world war. There were, it is true, movements of minor and often local importance, such as Futurism in Italy, Die neue Sachlichkeit in Germany and Dadaism in Paris. But these movements proved their essential lack of real body and are already dead. Of recent years, however, another movement has grown up which has a significance more than ironical.

One may say that the original struggle began as a repudiation of the idea, so dear to the heart of Sir Joshua Reynolds, that great Art must be subservient to telling stories of the Heroic past or, by extension, telling stories of any kind whatever. From the repudiation of telling stories Art progressed rapidly to the repudiation of giving any kind of information at all, except that conveyed by the sensations ensuing from the contemplation of abstract colours and forms undefiled by representation of any sort. These abstract forms and colours were planned by the artist and are intended to convey effects analogous to his sub-conscious thoughts. They must not be looked on as merely pure decoration.

But having got rid of all traces of communicable subject-matter, Art suddenly revolted. The truth seems to be that very few artists find themselves content with the making of abstract images. The investigations of Galton on the limitations of the instinctive idea, already referred to on page 130, would seem to be confirmed by looking at the works of the abstractionists themselves. Most artists who have experimented with abstractions find them in the end unsatisfying. There is no natural repulsion from the portraying of natural objects—quite the contrary. The abstractionists are the ones who wish to impose unnatural limitations. Nevertheless large numbers of contemporary painters are dissatisfied with realism. They desire to be strange and different, and are still pushed on by the ferment of discovery and adventure which, so active during the last fifty years, now apparently has come to an end, finding, like Alexander, no more worlds to conquer.

Suddenly appear the surrealists, offering what looks like a new field for exploration, but—and here's the rub—only by repudiating all the grand theories which artists have been trying to make the world swallow during the last fifty years. The Post-impressionists and Cubists having proved by apparently irrefutable logic and practice that story-telling in Art is anathema and damnation, the most recent school of thought turns round and asserts as clamorously that the highest function of Art after all is story-telling.

Only—and here is the great difference between the surrealists and the old academicians of the '80's—the stories may by no means be historical, romantic or sentimental, but only may be stories of the sub-conscious mind. The artist must be prepared to record any notion that pops into his head; he must exercise no selection, no control, no censorship. He is to be a disciple of Freud and Jung, and to become the visual recorder of the somersaults of his complexes, no matter what incongruities this may entail.

Unluckily the idea is not novel at all. It merely asserts that an artist has right to employ his phantasy, and phantasmal images must of necessity be sub-conscious. A small book by the German poet, Wilhelm Michel, " Die Grotesque in der Kunst," published before the war, gives us numerous examples of phantasmagorial Art from the earliest times onward, Art which has now belatedly been christened and advertised as surrealism. Only of course from a commercial and publicist point of view the tying up to a definite label and the attachment to a school of occult-scientific investigation is of considerable value.

Although surrealism has nothing to do with the fundamental processes of Art and reverts once more to the " despicable " story-telling, although surrealism deliberately deserts what is commonly called sanity, and, exploring the fringes of the sub-conscious mind, produces images that are only paralleled by those produced in lunatic asylums, it does actually bring a waft of common sense into this question of what is and what is not germane to the matter of pictorial Art.

During the last fifty years we have seen successively almost everything that we thought not to be Art proved to be Art, and now we have seen almost everything that was proved not to be Art proved to be Art after all. Is this a *reductio ad absurdum*? Not quite.

What has been eventually shown is that the boundaries of pictorial Art are far wider and more comprehensive than we have been prepared to admit. In fact, we must come to the final conclusion that everything and anything which can be better explained and made clear by an image, photographed, drawn, painted or sculptured, as long as it is produced and controlled by human intelligence, belongs to the province of pictorial Art.

As long as the essential properties of pictorial Art are satisfied, as long as line, form and colour are wrought together into a coherent and satisfactory whole, and are used not only to heighten the subject-matter, whether it be concrete or abstract, but also to become things of value in themselves, so long is the work that contains them a work of Art. And every school of artist and every form of Art as long as it fulfils the necessary conditions, has as much right to exist and be practised as any other school of Art. The only categorical " must " in the matter is that the wielder of the brush, pencil or chisel *must* be an artist. And there is no possible argument that can *prove* the presence of the artist ; only the accumulating approval of the sensitive audience and the slow weeding out of Time will say in what proportions our private judgments have been true or mistaken.

SALVADOR DALI

LA PERSISTANCE DE LA MÉMOIRE

CHAPTER XVIII

CONCLUSION

MODERN art in its first three principal exponents, Cézanne, Seurat, and Van Gogh, exhibits at once the characteristics which have governed its development. This is in harmony with the idea suggested that humanity moves on in steps or sudden progressions, alternating with quieter periods during which the full effects of the progression are assimilated. Cézanne implies all that has subsequently come out of technical self-consciousness, he has set artists working at their art with an almost scientific knowledge of how the material which is being shaped will react as a completed whole. The difference between artists of to-day and those of yesterday can be likened to that between a man driving a traction-engine and a man driving a horse : the man with the engine is a conscious master of his machine, the man with the horse is only a semi-conscious master.

Van Gogh, on the other hand, implies the liberation of the spirit. He represents, if you will, Anarchy ; but it is the sublime anarchy of a prophet, an anarchy in which each is to seek the highest good, defiant of rules which would keep him mediocre. Cézanne ends logically in Braque and abstraction. Van Gogh ends logically in Picasso, Kley and the surrealists. But logical conclusions may be a little difficult for humanity to swallow ; nor, indeed, is it necessary that logical conclusions are right. After all, the logical conclusion is only the logical conclusion of one aspect, it must neglect a host of other points of view. Human existence is possible because we are not very receptive to logical but prefer harmonized or balanced conclusions.

173

Between these two extremes we find a number of balanced conclusions, each of which can be considered as right from its own point of view, but none of which necessarily will control alone the rise of future genius.   But already out of the meeting-place of these conclusions, the Independents and the Salon d'Automne, one can see the birth of a new academism.   The old academism was that of Raphael, the new is that of Cézanne.   We can imagine the art world as a grandfather's clock; the pendulum ticks steadily, the hands progress.   Suddenly somebody gives the pendulum an extra swing.   For a while the ticking gallops, but at last the pendulum settles down once more to its steady movement.   Cézanne and the early group can be considered as the extra push on the pendulum : the Fauves and Cubists represent the agitated minutes which follow.   But already one can hear the clear tick-tack reasserting itself.

One can assert almost with confidence that the public may expect no new shocks for a very long while.   New genius will arise of course, but it will be within the limits of the new tradition.   If the public can assimilate all that it has recently received, it will be able to assimilate all that it will receive for a century or so.

In a way, academism may be considered as a good thing, as long as it is a living academism.   The Egyptians, the Gothics and so on, were academic artists.   By means of academism the artist can draw upon a reserve of force greater than his own.   Individualism is, at best, a weak thing.   The individual is one man against the world ; the academic has the world behind him.   The builders of Babel as academics were raising their tower against the high places of God. He merely reduced them to individualism and the danger was over.

But the academism of the past era, the Raphaelistic academy, had a weakness.   It was founded upon the idea that nature and that our vision of nature was a stable vision, also it became merged with sentimentality.   In Egypt each succeeding genius, sculptor or architect, reaffirmed or subtilized the academism of Egypt.   But with an academism of nature + Raphael each succeeding genius denies one part of the basis.   Rembrandt denies Raphael, Velazquez

GONTCHAROVA
SPRING

denies Raphael, Watteau denies Raphael, and so on. Thus the academism is weakened and at least becomes only a moribund tradition.

Will it be possible to erect a new living classicism upon the new foundations we have made ? Will critics and public cease to look at the individual in order to regard the universal ? That is the question. And upon the answer to this question depends the future of Twentieth Century Art.

INDEX

N

THE END

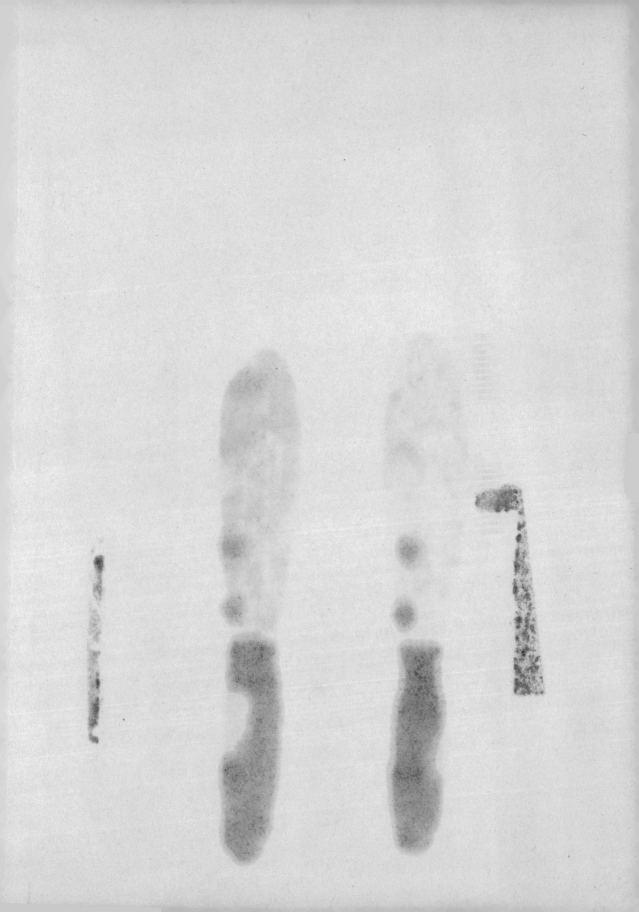

DATE DUE

GAYLORD   PRINTED IN U.S.A.